ISLAM

৩।৫১

ISLAM

A Concise Introduction

HUSTON SMITH

HarperSanFrancisco
A Division of HarperCollins*Publishers*

HarperCollins books may be purchased for educational, business, or sales promotional use. For information please write: Special Markets Department, HarperCollins Publishers, Inc., 10 East 53rd Street, New York, NY 10022.

HarperCollins Web site: http://www.harpercollins.com
HarperCollins®, ☕®, and HarperSanFrancisco™ are
trademarks of HarperCollins Publishers, Inc.

FIRST EDITION

ISBN 0-06-009557-1

03 04 05 06 ❖/RRD 10 9 8 7 6 5 4

CONTENTS

INTRODUCTION

This book lifts the chapter on Islam from my *The World's Religions* and publishes it as a small, free-standing book to help satisfy the hunger in America today for knowledge of this global faith. There is reason for this hunger. There are an estimated 1.2 billion Muslims in the world today — one out of every five persons on our planet is a Muslim — and Islam is probably the world's fastest growing religion. And it is no longer, strictly speaking, a foreign religion. There are somewhere between four and seven million Muslims who are United States citizens, which means that they already outnumber Episcopalians and Presbyterians, and their proportion in relation to other denominations is growing.

The chief reason for the spike in interest in this religion, however, is its involvement in the toppling of the World Trade Building and the strike on the Pentagon in September 2001. What kind of religion could be involved in terror of these proportions?

This book does not speak directly to that question; it provides background information for those who ask it. Islam has been around for fourteen centuries, and if civilization manages to survive will be around for as many more. It is the foundations of this faith that this book places in the reader's hands.

Those foundations need to be understood, and currently in the West they are not. No one has pointed this out more tellingly than columnist Meg Greenfield in 1979, when the Ayatolla

Khomani seized the American embassy in Iran and held 21 Americans hostage. As her words are even more apposite today than they were then, I will quote two paragraphs from them.

We are heading into an expansion of American involvement with that complex of religion, culture and geography known as Islam. There are two things to be said about this. One is that no part of the world is more important to our own well-being at this moment — and probably for the foreseeable future. The other is that no part of the world is more hopelessly, systematically and stubbornly misunderstood by us.

Why is this? In part, because it is virtually impossible for us to understand a world in which religious and civil power are thought to be the same. We are just not able to imagine the circumstances in which we would lodge religious beliefs not only at the center of our individual conduct, but also at the center of our politics.

Truer words were never spoken, and it would be presumptuous to think that this small book will dispel that misunderstanding. But it can do something toward dispelling three stereotypes about Islam, and to that end I will devote the remainder of this introduction.

The first stereotype concerns violence. The popular Western image of Islam is that it is the most violent of the great religions, but neither the Koran nor history support this view. The Koran contains 192 references to Allah's forbearance and mercy, as compared with 17 references to his judgment and wrath; and though there are violent injunctions in the Koran, they do not outweigh their counterparts in the Bible. Moreover (a point that is often overlooked by commentators who quote the Koranic passages out of context), they relate specifically to occasions when Muhammad was fighting for the life of the revelation that had been entrusted to him. Muslims have continued to fight over the centuries — tragically, wars scar the history of all religions — but I shall leave assessing the record to Norman Daniel, whose *Islam and the West: The Making of an Image*, is the most serious attempt that has been made to compare the use of force in Islam and

Christianity. His conclusion is that what can be safely said is that Islam has resorted to violence no more than has Christianity, while adding that that is probably a conservative estimate. As an example he points to Spain and Anatolia which changed hands at about the same time. In Spain Christians killed, expelled, or forced conversion on every Jew and Muslim in the land, whereas the seat of Orthodox Christianity remains in Constantinople to this very day.

Continuing in my own voice, the word *Islam* means explicitly "surrender," but it is related to the Arabic word *salam*, meaning "peace," as in the standard Islamic salutation *as-salamu 'alaykum*, peace be upon you. And when a virtuous Muslim enters heaven, it is said, the only word he will be able to utter for three days, over and over, is "peace," so overwhelmed will he be by the total realization of the condition he has been longing for his entire life. Between the bookends of Islam's name and its complete realization in paradise stands history, and it is instructive.

When the Prophet Muhammad brought the Koranic revelation to 7th century Arabia, a major part of his mission was to bring to an end the inter-tribal warfare that was wreaking havoc in the region. Pre-Islamic Arabia was caught up in vicious cycles of warfare wherein tribes fought one another in vendettas and revenge. At the start the Prophet and his cohorts had themselves to fight in order to survive, but once their foothold was secure, Muhammad turned his attention to building peaceful coalitions between tribes, so successfully that when he died he left as his political legacy a solidly united Arabia. And into warfare the Prophet introduced chivalry. No holds were barred in pre-Koranic warfare, but Muhammad introduced many traditions of forbearance. Agreements are to be honored and treachery avoided. The wounded are not to be mutilated nor the dead disfigured. Women, children and the old are to be spared, as are orchards, crops, and sacred objects — no scorched land policy or leveling of Hindu temples in Koranic Islam.

The key and inflammatory issue, though, is *jihad*. Literally the word means only effort, exertion or struggle, but it has taken on the meaning of Holy War. No full-fledged religion has been able to manage without a doctrine something like this — complete pacifism remains for smallish sects such as the Menonites and Quakers. Naked aggression must be halted and murder, pillage, and rape defended against. So far, so good. What is not good is that *jihad* has been turned by outsiders into a rallying cry for hatred against Islam — mention of the word conjures images of mobs streaming through streets destroying everything in sight — while within Islam fundamentalists seize on *jihad* as a rallying cry for their political ends. The truth of the matter is that Islam's concept of Holy War is virtually identical with the Just War doctrine in Christian canon law, right down to the notion that martyrs in both are assured of entry into heaven. In both cases the war must be defensive or to right a manifest wrong. Chivalry must be observed and the least possible damage inflicted to secure the end in question. And hostilities must cease when the objective is accomplished. Retaliation is forbidden.

So, to face the hard question, were the destructive acts of September 2001 *jihad*? If the perpetrators saw those acts as responses to, first, continuing Israeli settlement of the West Bank, and second, the boycott cordon around Iraq and daily unmanned bombing of her territory, both regarded as acts of aggression against *dar al-islam*, the House of Islam—to repeat, if the perpetrators of the damage saw their acts as responses to what they saw as aggression, they doubtless saw themselves as waging *jihad*. Otherwise it was mass murder.

On the second point of misunderstanding, the place of women in Islam, I can be brief. As I write these lines (October 2001) the treatment of women in Afghanistan is as inhumane as can be imagined, but that has nothing to do with Islam. One of the most important principles in trying to understand another religion is to distinguish between its defining features and the cultural baggage it has picked up along the way. One of the times this distinction was brought home to me was when I was looking into the differences between the Protestant and Russian Orthodox missionary approaches to the Alaskan Eskimos. The Russian missionaries adapted the Christian message to Eskimo culture in every way possible. They learned its languages, adopted Eskimo dress, and even incorporated local deities into the Christian angelic pantheon. By contrast, the Protestant missionaries seemed bent on Americanizing their converts in the process of Christianizing them — teaching them English, dressing them in business suits, the works. Coming upon this second group of converts, a stranger who was ignorant in these matters might easily have assumed that western garb was an ingredient of being Christian.

The actual status of women in the Koran bears no resemblance to the western stereotype, which is woven mostly of local customs that Muslims have assimilated. Muhammad's wife was educated, intelligent, and a highly successful business woman. Actually this issue can be resolved quite simply. I suspect that many of us know Muslim women who hold important positions in American society — my roster includes a physician, a teacher, a television director and a successful shopkeeper — who feel no conflict between their religion and their position in western society.

One of my favorite sayings of the Prophet that has received little notice has at least an indirect bearing here, so I will use it to round off this section on women. On one occasion a companion of the Prophet heard a bystander ask him, "Who is most entitled to my good conduct?" The Prophet replied, "Your mother." "Then whom?," the man asked. Again the Prophet answered, "Your mother." The question was repeated a third time and received the same answer. It was only when the questioner asked his question a fourth time that the Prophet said, "Your father."

Finally, fundamentalism. Islamic fundamentalism is very

different from Christian. Both share as their root cause the sense of being threatened, but by different things. Christian fundamentalism took shape in the early 20ᵗʰ century as a reaction against the threat (as seen by conservative Christians) of, first, Darwinian evolution which seemed to challenge the Biblical teaching that human beings were created directly by God; and second, the threat of "the higher criticism" which applied the tools of literary criticism to analyze the Bible as if it were any other book.

Islamic fundamentalism centers in the Middle East. The reason it flourishes there is that 80% of the Muslims are traditional in their outlook and way of life, while the 20% that rule them have been educated in the West and are modern in their life style and views. It takes no great feat of imagination to sense the threat the traditional majority feel from the ruling minority, and it causes them to dig in their heels. Two worlds, the old and the new, are in sharp collision.

The permutations of this conflict vary from region to region and are far too complex to enter into here. Moreover, to enter that domain would run counter to the intent of this introduction. I have used it to say a few words about several issues that are bound to be in the reader's mind since the September 2001 atrocities, but nothing has happened to alter the foundations of this faith. Those foundations must provide the background for everything else one says about Islam, and to my knowledge they are presented accurately in the pages that follow.

Huston Smith
Berkeley, California
February, 2002

PROLOGUE

We can begin with an anomaly. Of all the non-Western religions, Islam stands closest to the West—closest geographically, and also closest ideologically; for religiously it stands in the Abrahamic family of religions, while philosophically it builds on the Greeks. Yet despite this mental and spatial proximity, Islam is the most difficult religion for the West to understand. "No part of the world," an American columnist has written, "is more hopelessly and systematically and stubbornly misunderstood by us than that complex of religion, culture and geography known as Islam."[1]

This is ironic, but the irony is easily explained. Proximity is no guarantee of concord—tragically, more homicides occur within families than anywhere else. Islam and the West are neighbors. Common borders have given rise to border disputes, which, beginning with raids and counterraids, have escalated into vendettas, blood feuds, and all-out war. There is a happier side; in times and places Christians, Muslims, and Jews have lived together harmoniously—one thinks of Moorish Spain. But for a good part of the last fourteen hundred years, Islam and Europe have been at war, and people seldom have a fair picture of their enemies.[2] Islam is going to be an interesting religion for this book to negotiate.

Mistakes begin with its very name. Until recently it was called Muhammadanism by the West, which is not only inaccurate but offensive. It is inaccurate, Muslims say, because Muhammad didn't create this religion; God did—Muhammad was merely God's mouthpiece. Beyond this, the title is offensive because it conveys the impression that Islam focuses on a man rather than on God. To name Christianity after Christ is appropriate, they say, for Christians believe that Christ was God. But to call Islam Muhammadanism is like calling Christianity St. Paulism. The proper name of this religion is Islam. Derived from the root s-l-m, which means primarily "peace" but in a secondary sense "surrender," its full connotation is "the peace that comes when one's life is surrendered to God." This makes Islam—together with Buddhism, from *budh*, awakening—one of the two religions that is named after the attribute it seeks to cultivate; in Islam's case, life's total surrender to God. Those who adhere to Islam are known as Muslims.

— 1 —

ISLAMIC
BACKGROUND

"Around the name of the Arabs,"writes Philip Hitti, "gleams that halo which belongs to the world-conquerors. Within a century after their rise this people became the masters of an empire extending from the shores of the Atlantic Ocean to the confines of China, an empire greater than that of Rome at its zenith. In this period of unprecedented expansion, they assimilated to their creed, speech, and even physical type, more aliens than any stock before or since, not excepting the Hellenic, the Roman, the Anglo-Saxon, or the Russian.[1]

Central in this Arab rise to greatness was their religion, Islam. If we ask how it came into being, the outsider's answer points to socioreligious currents that were playing over Arabia in Muhammad's day and uses them to explain what happened. The Muslims' answer is different. Islam begins not with Muhammad in sixth-century Arabia, they say, but with God. "In the beginning God . . ." the book of Genesis tells us. The Koran agrees. It differs only in using the word *Allah*. Allah is formed by joining the definite article *al* (meaning "the") with *Ilah* (God). Literally, Allah means "the God." Not *a* god, for there is only one. *The* God. When the masculine plural ending *im* is dropped from the Hebrew word for God, *Elohim*, the two words sound much alike.

God created the world, and after it human beings. The name of the first man was Adam. The descendants of Adam led to Noah, who had a son named Shem. This is where the word Semite comes from; literally a Semite is a descendant of Shem. Like the Jews, the Arabs consider themselves a Semitic people. The descendants of Shem led to Abraham, and so far we are still in the tradition of Judaism and Christianity. Indeed, it was the submission of Abraham in his supreme test—would he be willing to sacrifice his son Ishmael?—that appears to have provided Islam with its name. Abraham married Sarah. Sarah had no son, so Abraham, wanting to continue his line, took Hagar for his second wife. Hagar bore him a son, Ishmael, whereupon Sarah conceived and likewise had a son, named Isaac. Sarah then demanded that Abraham banish Ishmael and Hagar from the tribe. Here we come to the first divergence between the koranic and biblical accounts. According to the Koran, Ishmael went to the place where Mecca was to rise. His descendants, flourishing in Arabia, became Muslims; whereas those of Isaac, who remained in Palestine, were Hebrews and became Jews.

— 2 —

THE SEAL OF
THE PROPHETS

Following Ishmael's line in Arabia, we come in the latter half of the sixth century A.D. to Muhammad, the prophet through whom Islam reached its definitive form, Muslims believe. There had been authentic prophets of God before him, but he was their culmination; hence he is called "The Seal of the Prophets." No valid prophets will follow him.

The world into which Muhammad was born is described by subsequent Muslims in a single word: ignorant. Life under the conditions of the desert had never been serene. People felt almost no obligation to anyone outside their tribes. Scarcity of material goods made brigandage a regional institution and the proof of virility. In the sixth century political deadlock and the collapse of the magistrate in the leading city of Mecca aggravated this generally chaotic situation.

Drunken orgies were commonplace, and the gaming impulse uncontrolled. The prevailing religion watched from the sidelines, providing no check. Best described as an animistic polytheism, it peopled the sandy wastes with beastly sprites called *jinn* or demons. Fantastic personifications of desert terrors, they inspired neither exalted sentiments nor moral restraint. Conditions could hardly have been better calculated to produce a smoldering undercurrent, which erupted in sudden affrays and blood feuds, some of which extended for half a century. The times called for a deliverer.

He was born into the leading tribe of Mecca, the Koreish, in approximately A.D. 570, and was named Muhammad, "highly praised," which name has since been borne by more male children than any other in the world. His early life was cradled in tragedy, for his father died a few days before he was born, his mother when he was six, and his grandfather, who cared for him after his mother's death, when he was eight. Thereafter he was adopted into his uncle's home. Though the latter's declining fortunes forced the young orphan to work hard minding his uncle's flocks, he was warmly received by his new family. The angels of God, we are told, had opened Muhammad's heart and filled it with light.

The description epitomizes his early character as this comes down to us by tradition. Pure-hearted and beloved in his circle, he was, it is said, of sweet and gentle disposition. His bereavements having made him sensitive to human suffering in every form, he was always ready to help others, especially the poor and the weak. His sense of honor, duty, and fidelity won him, as he grew older, the high and enviable titles of "The True," "The Upright," "The Trustworthy One." Yet despite his concern for others, he remained removed from them in outlook and ways, isolated in a corrupt and degenerate society. As he grew from childhood to youth and from youth to manhood, the lawless strife of his contemporaries, the repeated outbursts of pointless quarrels among tribes frequenting the Meccan fairs, and the general immorality and cynicism of his day combined to produce in the prophet-to-be a reaction of horror and disgust. Silently, broodingly, his thoughts were turning inward.

Upon reaching maturity he took up the caravan business, and at the age of twenty-five entered the service of a wealthy widow named Khadija. His prudence and integrity impressed her greatly, and gradually their relation deepened into affection, then love. Though she was fifteen years his senior, they were married and the match proved happy in every respect. During a long, desolate period that lay ahead, in which no one would believe in him, not even himself, Khadija was to remain steadfastly by his side, consoling him and tending hope's thin flame. "God," tradition was to record, "comforted him through her, for she made his burden light."

Following his marriage were fifteen years of preparation before his ministry was to begin. A mountain on the outskirts of Mecca, known as Mount Hira, contained a cave, and Muhammad, needing solitude, began to frequent it. Peering into the mysteries of good and evil, unable to accept the crudeness, superstition, and fratricide that were accepted as normal, "this great fiery heart, seething, simmering like a great furnace of thoughts," was reaching out for God.[1]

The desert *jinn* were irrelevant to this quest, but one deity was not. Named Allah[2] he was worshiped by the Meccans not as the only God but as an impressive one nonetheless. Creator, supreme provider, and determiner of human destiny, he was capable of inspiring authentic religious feeling and genuine devotion. Certain contemplatives of the time, called *hanifs*, worshiped Allah exclusively, and Muhammad was one of their number. Through vigils, often lasting the entire night, Allah's reality became for Muhammad increasingly evident and awesome. Fearful and wonderful, real as life, real as death, real as the universe he had ordained, Allah (Muhammad was convinced) was far greater than his countrymen supposed. This God, whose majesty overflowed a desert cave to fill all heaven and earth, was surely not a god or even the greatest of gods. He was what his name literally claimed: He was *the* God, One and only, One without rival. Soon from this mountain cave was to sound the greatest phrase of the Arabic language; the deep, electrifying cry that was to rally a people and explode their power to the limits of the known world: *La ilaha illa 'llah!* There is no god but God!

But first the prophet must receive, around 610, his commission. Gradually, as Muhammad's visits to the cave became more compelling, the command that he later saw as predestined took form. It was the same command that had fallen earlier on Abraham, Moses, Samuel, Isaiah, and Jesus. Wherever, whenever, this call comes, its form may differ but its essence is the same. A voice falls from heaven saying, "You are the appointed one." On the Night of Power, as a strange peace pervaded creation and all nature was turned toward its Lord, in the middle of that night, say the Muslims, the Book was opened to a ready soul. Some add that on the anniversary of that Night it is possible to hear the grass grow and the trees speak, and that those who do so become saints or sages, for on the annual return of that Night one can see through the fingers of God.[3]

On that first Night of Power, as Muhammad lay on the floor of the cave, his mind locked in deepest contemplation, there came to him an angel in the form of a man. The angel said to him: "Proclaim!"[4] and he said: "I am not a proclaimer"; whereupon, as Muhammad was himself to report, "the Angel took me and whelmed me in his embrace until he had reached the limit of my endurance. Then he released me and said again, 'Proclaim!' Again I said: 'I am not a proclaimer,' and again he whelmed me in his embrace. When again he had reached the limit of my endurance he said 'Proclaim!,' and when I again protested, he whelmed me for a third time, this time saying:

> Proclaim in the name of your Lord who created!
> Created man from a clot of blood.
> Proclaim: Your Lord is the Most Generous,
> Who teaches by the pen;
> Teaches man what he knew not."
>
> (Koran 96:1–3)

Arousing from his trance, Muhammad felt as if the words he had heard had been branded on his soul. Terrified, he rushed home and fell into paroxysms. Coming to himself, he told Khadija that he had become either a prophet or "one possessed—mad." At first she resisted this disjunction, but on hearing his full story she became his first convert—which, Muslims often remark, in itself speaks well for his authenticity, for if anyone understands a man's true character it is his wife. "Rejoice, O dear husband, and be of good cheer," she said. "You will be the Prophet of this people."

We can imagine the spiritual anguish, the mental

doubts, the waves of misgivings that followed in the wake of the experience. Was the voice really God's? Would it come again? Above all, what would it require?

It returned repeatedly, and its command was always the same—to proclaim. "O thou, inwrapped in thy mantle, arise and warn, and glorify thy Lord." Muhammad's life was no more his own. From that time forth it was given to God and to humanity, preaching with unswerving purpose in the face of relentless persecution, insult, and outrage, the words that God was to transmit for twenty-three years.

The content of the revelation will be reserved for later sections. Here we need only speak of the response it drew and note that its appeal throughout was to human reason as vectored by religious discernment.

In an age charged with supernaturalism, when miracles were accepted as the stock-in-trade of the most ordinary saint, Muhammad refused to pander to human credulity. To miracle-hungry idolaters seeking signs and portents, he cut the issue clean: "God has not sent me to work wonders; He has sent me to preach to you. My Lord; be praised! Am I more than a man sent as an apostle?"[5] From first to last he resisted every impulse to inflate his own image. "I never said that God's treasures are in my hand, that I knew the hidden things, or that I was an angel. I am only a preacher of God's words, the bringer of God's message to mankind."⁶ If signs be sought, let them be not of Muhammad's greatness but of God's, and for these one need only open one's eyes. The heavenly bodies holding their swift, silent course in the vault of heaven, the incredible order of the universe, the rain that falls to relieve the parched earth, palms bending with golden fruit, ships that glide across the seas laden with goodness—can these be the handiwork of gods of stone? What fools to cry for signs when creation tokens nothing else! In an age of credulity, Muhammad taught respect for the world's incontrovertible order, a respect that was to bring Muslims to science before it did Christians. Apart from his nocturnal ascent through the heavens, which will be mentioned, he claimed only one miracle, that of the Koran itself. That he with his own resources could have produced such truth—this was the one naturalistic hypothesis he could not accept.

As for the reaction to his message, it was (for all but a few) violently hostile. The reasons for the hostility can be reduced to three: (1) Its uncompromising monotheism threatened polytheistic beliefs and the considerable revenue that was coming to Mecca from pilgrimages to its 360 shrines (one for every day of the lunar year); (2) its moral teachings demanded an end to the licentiousness that citizens clung to; and (3) its social content challenged an unjust order. In a society riven with class distinctions, the new Prophet was preaching a message that was intensely democratic. He was insisting that in the sight of his Lord all people were equal.

As such a teaching suited neither their tastes nor their privileges, the Meccan leaders were determined to have none of it. They began their attack with ridicule: pinpricks of laughter, petty insults, and hoots of derision. When these proved ineffective, their words turned uglier—to abuse, calumny, vilification, and then overt threats. When these too failed, they resorted to open persecution. They covered Muhammad and his followers with dirt and filth as they were praying. They pelted them with stones, beat them with sticks, threw them in prison, and tried to starve them out by refusing to sell to them. To no avail; persecution only steeled the will of Muhammad's followers. "Never since the days when primitive Christianity startled the world from its sleep," wrote a scholar whose words assume added weight because he was on the whole a severe critic of Islam, "had men seen the like arousing of spiritual life—of faith that suffers sacrifices."[7] Muhammad himself set the pattern for their fidelity. Under the most perilous of circumstances, he continued to throw heart and soul into his preaching, adjuring listeners wherever he could find them to abandon their evil ways and prepare for the day of reckoning.

At first the odds were so heavily against him that he made few converts; three long years of heartbreaking effort yielded less than forty. But his enemies could do nothing to forever seal the hearts of the Meccans against his words. Slowly but steadily, people of energy, talent, and worth became convinced of the truth of his message until, by the end of a decade, several hundred families were acclaiming him as God's authentic spokesman.

3

THE MIGRATION
THAT LED TO VICTORY

B y this time the Meccan nobility was alarmed. What had begun as a pretentious prophetic claim on the part of a half-crazed camel driver had turned into a serious revolutionary movement that was threatening their very existence. They were determined to rid themselves of the troublemaker for good.

As he faced this severest crisis of his career, Muhammad was suddenly waited on by a delegation of the leading citizens of Yathrib, a city 280 miles to Mecca's north. Through pilgrims and other visitors to Mecca, Muhammad's teachings had won a firm hold in Yathrib. The city was facing internal rivalries that put it in need of a strong leader from without, and Muhammad looked like the man. After receiving a delegation's pledge that they would worship Allah only, that they would observe the precepts of Islam, and that they would obey its prophet in all that was

right and defend him and his adherents as they would
their women and children, Muhammad received a
sign from God to accept the charge. About seventy
families preceded him. When the Meccan leaders got
wind of the exodus they did everything in their power
to prevent his going; but, together with his close companion Abu Bakr, he eluded their watch and set out for
Yathrib, taking refuge on the way in a crevice south of
the city. Horsemen scouring the countryside came so
close to discovering them that Muhammad's companion was moved to despair. "We are only two," he mur-
mured. "No, we are three," Muhammad answered, "for
God is with us." The Koran agrees. "He was with them,"
it observes, for they were not discovered. After three
days, when the search had slackened, they managed to
procure two camels and make their hazardous way by
unfrequented paths to the city of their destination.

The year was 622. The migration, known in Arabic
as the *Hijra*, is regarded by Muslims as the turning
point in world history and is the year from which they
date their calendar. Yathrib soon came to be known as
Medinat al-Nabi, the City of the Prophet, and then by
contraction simply to Medina, "the city."

From the moment of his arrival at Medina,
Muhammad assumed a different role. From prophecy
he was pressed into administration. The despised
preacher became a masterful politician; the prophet
was transformed into statesman. We see him as the

master not merely of the hearts of a handful of devotees but of the collective life of a city, its judge and general as well as its teacher.

Even his detractors concede that he played his new role brilliantly. Faced with problems of extraordinary complexity, he proved to be a remarkable statesman. As the supreme magistrate, he continued to lead as unpretentious a life as he had in the days of his obscurity. He lived in an ordinary clay house, milked his own goats, and was accessible day and night to the humblest in his community. Often seen mending his own clothes, "no emperor with his tiaras was obeyed as this man in a cloak of his own clouting."[1] God, say Muslim historians, put before him the key to the treasures of this world, but he refused it.

Tradition depicts his administration as an ideal blend of justice and mercy. As chief of state and trustee of the life and liberty of his people, he exercised the justice necessary for order, meting out punishment to those who were guilty. When the injury was toward himself, on the other hand, he was gentle and merciful even to his enemies. In all, the Medinese found him a master whom it was as difficult not to love as not to obey. For he had, as one biographer has written, "the gift of influencing men, and he had the nobility only to influence for the good."[2]

For the remaining ten years of his life, his personal history merged with that of the Medinese commonwealth of which he was the center. Exercising superb statecraft, he welded the five heterogeneous and conflicting tribes of the city, three of which were Jewish, into an orderly confederation. The task was not an easy one, but in the end he succeeded in awakening in the citizens a spirit of cooperation unknown in the city's history. His reputation spread and people began to flock from every part of Arabia to see the man who had wrought this "miracle."

There followed the struggle with the Meccans for the mind of Arabia as a whole. In the second year of the *Hijra* the Medinese won a spectacular victory over a Meccan army many times larger, and they interpreted the victory as a clear sign that the angels of heaven were battling on their side. The following year, however, witnessed a reversal during which Muhammad himself was wounded. The Meccans did not follow up their victory until two years later, when they laid siege to Medina in a last desperate effort to force the Muslims to capitulate. The failure of this effort turned the tide permanently in Muhammad's favor; and within three years—eight years after his Migration from Mecca—he who had left as a fugitive returned as conqueror. The city that had treated him cruelly now lay at his feet, with his former persecutors at his mercy. Typically, however, he did not press his victory. In the hour of his triumph the past was forgiven. Making his way to the famous Ka'ba, a cubical temple (said to have been built by Abraham) that Muhammad rededicated to Allah and adopted as Islam's focus, he accepted the virtual mass conversion of the city. Himself, he returned to Medina.

Two years later, in A.D. 632 (10 A.H., After the *Hijra*), Muhammad died with virtually all of Arabia under his control. With all the power of armies and police, no other Arab had ever succeeded in uniting his countrymen as he had. Before the century closed his followers had conquered Armenia, Persia, Syria, Palestine, Iraq, North Africa, and Spain, and had crossed the Pyrenees into France. But for their defeat by Charles Martel in the Battle of Tours in 733, the entire Western world might today be Muslim. Within a brief span of mortal life, Muhammad had "called forth out of unpromising material a nation never united before, in a country that was hitherto but a geographical expression; established a religion which in vast areas superseded Christianity and Judaism and still claims the adherence of a goodly portion of the human race; and laid the basis of an empire that was soon to embrace within its far-flung boundaries the fairest provinces of the then civilized world."[3]

In *The 100: A Ranking of the Most Influential Persons in History*, Michael Hart places Muhammad first. His "unparalleled combination of secular and religious influence entitles Muhammad to be considered the most influential single figure in human history," Hart writes.[4] The explanation that Muslims give for that verdict is simple. The entire work, they say, was the work of God.

4

THE
STANDING MIRACLE

The blend of admiration, respect, and affection that the Muslim feels for Muhammad is an impressive fact of history. They see him as a man who experienced life in exceptional range. Not only was he a shepherd, merchant, hermit, exile, Soldier, lawmaker, prophet-priestking, and mystic; he was also an orphan, for many years the husband of one wife much older than himself, a many times bereaved father, a widower, and finally the husband of many wives, some much younger than himself. In all of these roles he was exemplary. All this is in the minds of Muslims as they add to the mention of his name the benediction, "Blessings and peace be upon him." Even so, they never mistake him for the earthly center of their faith. That place is reserved for the bible of Islam, the Koran.

Literally, the word *al-qur'an* in Arabic (and hence "koran,") means a recitation. Fulfilling that purpose, the Koran is perhaps the most recited (as well as read) book in the world. Certainly, it is the world's most memorized book, and possibly the one that exerts the most influence on those who read it. So great was Muhammad's regard for its contents that (as we have seen) he considered it the only major miracle God worked through him—God's "standing miracle," as he called it. That he himself, unschooled to the extent that he was unlettered *(ummi)* and could barely write his name, could have produced a book that provides the ground plan of all knowledge and at the same time is grammatically perfect and without poetic peer— this, Muhammad, and with him all Muslims, are convinced defies belief. He put the point in a rhetorical question: "Do you ask for a greater miracle than this, O unbelieving people, than to have your language chosen as the language of that incomparable Book, one piece of which puts all your golden poetry to shame?"

Four-fifths the length of the New Testament, the Koran is divided into 114 chapters or *surahs*, which (with the exception of the short first chapter that figures in the Muslim's daily prayers) are arranged in order of decreasing length. Thus Surah Two has 286 verses, Surah Three has 200, down to Surah One Hundred Fourteen, which has only six.

Muslims tend to read the Koran literally. They consider it the earthly facsimile of an Uncreated Koran in almost exactly the way that Christians consider Jesus to have been the human incarnation of God. The comparison that reads, "If Christ is God incarnate, the Koran is God inlibriate" (from *liber*, Latin for book) is inelegant but not inaccurate. The created Koran is the instantiation, in letters and sounds, of the Koran's limitless essence in its Uncreated Form. Not that there are two Korans, of course. Rather, the created Koran is the formal crystallization of the infinite reality of the Uncreated Koran. Two levels of reality are operative here. There is the Divine Reality of the Uncreated Koran, and there is the earthly reality of the created Koran. When the created Koran is said to be a miracle, the miracle referred to is the presence of the Uncreated Koran within the letters and sounds of its created (and therefore necessarily in certain ways circumscribed) manifestation.

The words of the Koran came to Muhammad in manageable segments over twenty-three years through voices that seemed at first to vary and sometimes sounded like "the reverberating of bells," but which gradually condensed into a single voice that identified itself as Gabriel's. Muhammad had no control over the flow of the revelation; it descended on him independent of his will. When it arrived he was changed into a special state that was externally discernible. Both his appearance and the sound of his voice would change. He reported that the words assaulted him as if they were solid and heavy: "For We shall charge thee with a word of weight" (73:5; all such references in this chapter are to *surah* and verse[s] in the Koran). Once they descended while he was riding a camel. The animal sought vainly to support the added weight by adjusting its legs. By the time the revelation ceased, its belly was pressed against the earth and its legs splayed out. The words that Muhammad exclaimed in these often trance-like states were memorized by his followers and recorded on bones, bark, leaves, and scraps of parchment, with God preserving their accuracy throughout.

The Koran continues the Old and New Testaments, God's earlier revelations, and presents itself as their culmination: "We made a covenant of old with the Children of Israel [and] you have nothing of guidance until you observe the Torah and the Gospel" (5:70, 68). This entitles Jews and Christians to be included with Muslims as "People of the Book." (Because the context of the koranic revelation is the Middle East, religions of other lands are not mentioned, but their existence is implied and in principle validated, as in the following verses: "To every people we have sent a messenger . . . [Some] We have mentioned to you, and [some] we have not mentioned to you" [10:47, 4:164]). Nevertheless, Muslims regard the Old and New Testaments as sharing two defects from which the Koran is free. For circumstantial reasons they record only portions of Truth. Second, the Jewish and Christian Bibles were partially corrupted in transmission, a fact that explains the occasional discrepancies that occur between their accounts and parallel ones in the Koran. Exemption from these two limitations makes the Koran the final and infallible revelation of God's will. Its second chapter says explicitly: "This is the Scripture whereof there is no doubt."

From the outside things look otherwise, for from without the Koran is all but impenetrable. No one has ever curled up on a rainy weekend to read the Koran. Carlyle confessed that it was "as toilsome reading as I ever undertook; a wearisome, confused jumble, crude, incondite. Nothing but a sense of duty could carry any European through the Koran." Sir Edward Gibbon said much the same: "The European will peruse with impatience its endless incoherent rhapsody of fable and precept, and declamation, which seldom excites a sentiment or an idea, which sometimes crawls in the dust, and is sometimes lost in the clouds."[1] How are we to understand the discrepancy of the Koran as read from within and from without?

The language in which it was proclaimed, Arabic, provides an initial clue. "No people in the world," writes Philip Hitti, "are so moved by the word, spoken or written, as the Arabs. Hardly any language seems capable of exercising over the minds of its users such irresistible influence as Arabic." Crowds in Cairo, Damascus, or Baghdad can be stirred to the highest emotional pitch by statements that, when translated, seem banal. The rhythm, melodic cadence, the rhyme produce a powerful hypnotic effect. Thus the power of the koranic revelation lies not only in the literal meaning of its words but also in the language in which this meaning incorporated, including its sound. The Koran was from the first a vocal phenomenon; we remember that we are to "recite" in the name of the Lord! Because content and container are here inseparably fused, translations cannot possibly convey the emotion, the fervor, and the mystery that the Koran holds in the original. This is why, in sharp contrast to Christians, who have translated their Bible into every known script, Muslims have preferred to teach others the language in which they believe God spoke finally with incomparable force and directness.[2]

Language, however, is not the only barrier the Koran presents to outsiders, for in content too it is like no other religious text. Unlike the Upanishads, it is not explicitly metaphysical. It does not ground its theology in dramatic narratives as the Indian epics do, nor in historical ones as do the Hebrew scriptures; nor is God revealed in human form as in the Gospels and the *Bhagavad-Gita*. Confining ourselves to the Semitic scriptures, we can say that whereas the Old and New Testaments are directly historical and indirectly doctrinal, the Koran is directly doctrinal and indirectly historical. Because the overwhelming thrust of the Koran is to proclaim the unity, omnipotence, omniscience, and mercy of God—and correlatively the total dependence of human life upon him—historical facts are in its case merely reference points that have scarcely any interest in themselves. This explains why the prophets are cited without any chronological order; why historical occurrences are sometimes recounted so elliptically as to be unintelligible without commentaries; and why the biblical stories that the Koran refers to are presented in an unexpected, abbreviated, and dry manner. They are stripped of their epic character and inserted as didactic examples of the infinitely various things that declare God's praise. When the Lord-servant relationship is the essential point to get across, all else is but commentary and allusion.

Perhaps we shall be less inclined to fault the Koran for the strange face it presents to foreigners if we note that foreign scriptures present their own problems to Muslims. To speak only of the Old and New Testaments, Muslims express disappointment in finding that those texts do not take the form of Divine speech and merely report things that happened. In the Koran God speaks in the first person. Allah describes himself and makes known his laws. The Muslim is therefore inclined to consider each individual sentence of the Holy Book as a separate revelation and to experience the words themselves, even their sounds, as a means of grace. "The Qur'an does not document what is other than itself. It is not about the truth: it is the truth."[3] By contrast the Jewish and Christian Bibles seem more distant from God for placing religious meaning in reports of events instead of God's direct pronouncements.

The Koran's direct delivery creates, for the reader, a final problem that in other scriptures is eased by greater use of narrative and myth. One discerning commentator on the Koran puts this point as follows: "The seeming incoherence of the text has its cause in the incommensurable disproportion between the Spirit [Uncreated Koran] and the limited resources of human language. It is as though the poverty-stricken coagulation which is the language of mortal man were under the formidable pressure of the Heavenly Word broken into a thousand fragments, or as if God in order to express a thousand truths, had but a dozen words at his command and so was compelled to make use of allusions heavy with meaning, of ellipses, abridgements and symbolical syntheses."[4]

Putting comparisons behind us, it is impossible to overemphasize the central position of the Koran in the elaboration of any Islamic doctrine. With large portions memorized in childhood, it regulates the interpretation and evaluation of every event. It is a memorandum for the faithful, a reminder for daily doings, and a repository of revealed truth. It is a manual of definitions and guarantees, and at the same time a road map for the will. Finally, it is a collection of maxims to meditate on in private, deepening endlessly one's sense of the divine glory. "Perfect is the Word of your Lord in truth and justice" (6:115).

5

BASIC THEOLOGICAL CONCEPTS

With a few striking exceptions, which will be noted, the basic theological concepts of Islam are virtually identical with those of Judaism and Christianity, its forerunners. We shall confine our attention in this chapter to four that are the most important: God, Creation, the Human Self, and the Day of Judgment.

As in other historical religions, everything in Islam centers on its religious Ultimate, God. God is immaterial and therefore invisible. For the Arabs this cast no doubt on his reality, for they never succumbed to the temptation—sorely reinforced by modern materialistic attitudes—to regard only the visible as the real; one of the tributes the Koran pays to Muhammad is that "he did not begrudge the Unseen." As desert dwellers, the notion of invisible hands that drove the blasts that swept the desert and formed the deceptive mirages that lured the traveler to his destruction was always with them.

Thus the Koran did not introduce the Arab to the unseen world of spirit, nor even to monotheism, since certain sensitive souls known as *hanifs* had already moved to that position before Muhammad. Its innovation was to remove idols from the religious scene and focus the divine in a single invisible God for everyone. It is in this sense that the indelible contribution of Islam to Arabic religion was monotheism.

We must immediately add that Muslims see monotheism as Islam's contribution not simply to the Arabs but to religion in its entirety. Hinduism's prolific images are taken as proof that it never arrived at the worship of the single God. Judaism was correctly instructed through its *Shema*—"Hear O Israel, the Lord our God, the Lord is One"—but its teachings were confined to the people of Israel. Christians, for their part, compromised their monotheism by deifying Christ. Islam honors Jesus as a prophet and accepts his virgin birth; Adam's and Jesus' souls are the only two that God created directly.[1] The Koran draws the line at the doctrine of the Incarnation and the Trinity, however, seeing these as inventions that blur the Divine/human distinction. In the words of the Koran: "They say the God of mercy has begotten a son. Now have you uttered a grievous thing. . . . It is not proper for God to have children" (3:78, 19:93). Muslims are not fond of parental images for God, even when employed metaphorically. To speak of human beings as "God's children" casts God in too human a mode. It is anthropomorphic.

Turning to the koranic depiction of God's nature, the first thing that strikes us is its awesomeness, its fear-inspiring power. Verse 7:143 contains the koranic account of Moses' request to see God. When God showed himself instead to a neighboring mountain, thereby "sending it crashing down, Moses fell down senseless."[2]

Power of this order—it is infinite, for God is omnipotent—inspires fear, and it is fair to say that Muslims fear Allah. This, however, is not cringing fear in the face of a capricious tyrant. Rather, Muslims argue, it is the only appropriate emotion—any other involves denial in the technical, psychological sense of the word—when human beings face up to the magnitude of the consequences that follow from being on the right or wrong side of an uncompromisingly moral universe; one, moreover, in which beliefs and convictions are decisive because they generate actions. If nihilism is the dissipation of difference, a kind of moral leveling-out through entropy, Allah's universe is its exact opposite. Good and evil matter. Choices have consequences, and to disregard them would be as disastrous as climbing a mountain blindfolded. Belief in the Koran occupies the decisive place it does

because it is the analogue to a mountaineer's assess-
ment of Mount Everest: Its majesty is evident, but so
are the dangers it presents. Mistakes could be disastrous. Koranic images of heaven and hell are pressed
into full service here; but once we come to terms with
the fear that life's inbuilt precariousness inspires, other
lesser fears subside. The second, supporting root of the
word *islam* is peace.

It is important to remember this last point, because
the holy dread that Allah inspires led early Western
students of the Koran to think that it outstrips God's
mercy. Allah was seen to be a stern and wrathful judge,
domineering and ruthless. This is a clear misreading;
God's compassion and mercy are cited 192 times in the
Koran, as against 17 references to his wrath and
vengeance. He who is Lord of the worlds is also

> the Holy, the Peaceful, the Faithful, the Guardian over
> His servants, the Shelterer of the orphan, the Guide of
> the erring, the Deliverer from every affliction, the
> Friend of the bereaved, the Consoler of the afflicted; in
> His hand is good, and He is the generous Lord, the gra-
> cious, the Hearer, the Near-at-Hand, the Compas-
> sionate, the Merciful, the Very-forgiving, whose love for
> man is more tender than that of the mother-bird for her
> young.[3]

Thanks to Allah's mercy, the world of the Koran is

finally a world of joy. There is air, and sun, and confidence—not only in ultimate justice but also in help along the way and pardon for the contrite.

> *By the noonday brightness, and by the night when it darkens, your Lord has not forsaken you, neither has He been displeased. Surely the Hereafter shall be better for you than the past; and in the end He will be bounteous to you, and you will be satisfied. Did He not find you an orphan, and give you a home; erring, and guided you; needy, and enriched you?*
>
> (93:1–8)

Standing beneath God's gracious skies, the Muslim can at any moment lift heart and soul directly into the divine presence, there to receive both strength and guidance for life's troubled course. The access is open because, though the human and the divine are infinitely different, no barrier separates them.

> *Is He not closer than the vein of your neck? You need not raise your voice, for he knows the secret whisper, and what is yet more hidden. . . . He knows what is in the land and in the sea; no leaf falls but He knows it; nor is there a grain in the darkness under the earth, nor a thing, green or sere, but it is recorded.*
>
> (6:12, 59)

From God we can turn to Creation as our second theological concept. The Koran abounds in lyrical descriptions of the natural world. Here, though, the point is that that world is not presented as emerging from the divine by some process of inbuilt emanation, as Hindu texts suggest. It was created by a deliberate act of Allah's will: "He has created the heavens and the earth" (16:3). This fact carries two important consequences. First, the world of matter is both real and important. Herein lies one of the sources of Islamic science, which during Europe's Dark Ages flourished as nowhere else on earth. Second, being the handiwork of Allah, who is perfect in both goodness and power, the material world must likewise be good. "You do not see in the creation of the All-merciful any imperfection. Return your gaze. . . . It comes back to you dazzled" (67:4). Here we meet a confidence in the material aspects of life and existence that we will find shared by the other two Sernitically originated religions, Judaism and Christianity

Foremost among God's creations is the human self, whose nature, koranically defined, is our third doctrinal subject. "He has created man," we read in Surah 16:3, and the first thing that we note about this creation is its sound constitution. This could have been inferred, given its Maker, but the Koran states it explicitly: "Surely We have created humanity of the best stature" (95:4). The koranic word for human nature in its God-established original is *fitra,* and it has been stained by no catastrophic fall. The closest Islam comes to the Christian doctrine of original sin is in its concept of *ghaflah,* or forgetting. People do forget their divine origin, and this mistake needs repeatedly to be corrected. But their fundamental nature is unalterably good, so they are entitled to self-respect and a healthy self-image.

With life acknowledged as a gift from its Creator, we can turn to its obligations, which are two. The first of these is gratitude for the life that has been received. The Arabic word "infidel" is actually shaded more toward "one who lacks thankfulness" than one who disbelieves. The more gratitude one feels, the more natural it feels to let the bounty that has entered flow through one's life and on to others, for to hoard it would be as unnatural as trying to dam a waterfall. The ingrate, the Koran tells us, "covers" or "hides" God's blessings and thereby fails to enjoy the link with the Creator that every moment provides.

The second standing human obligation recalls us to the name of this religion. The opening paragraphs of this book informed us that *islam* means surrender, but we now need to probe this attribute more deeply.

Thoughts of surrender are so freighted with military connotations that it requires conscious effort to notice that surrender can mean a wholehearted giving of oneself—to a cause, or in friendship and love.

William James shows how central surrender is to all
religion.

> *When all is said and done, we are in the end absolutely
> dependent on the universe; and into sacrifices and sur-
> renders of some sort, deliberately looked at and accepted,
> we are drawn and pressed as into our only permanent
> positions of repose. Now in those states of mind which
> fall short of religion, the surrender is submitted to as an
> imposition of necessity, and the sacrifice is undergone at
> the very best without complaint. In the religious life,
> on the contrary, surrender and sacrifice are positively
> espoused: even unnecessary givings-up are added in
> order that the happiness may increase. Religion thus
> makes easy and felicitous what in any case is necessary.*[4]

To this account of surrender's virtues we can add in
Islamic parlance that to be a slave to Allah is to be freed
from other forms of slavery—ones that are degrading,
such as slavery to greed, or to anxiety, or to the desire
for personal status. It also helps here if we alternate the
word "surrender" with "commitment"; for in addition
to being exempt from military associations, commitment suggests moving toward rather than giving up. In
this reading Islam emerges as a religion that aims at
total commitment; commitment in which nothing is
withheld from the Divine. This explains why Abraham
is by far the most important figure in the Koran, for he

passed the ultimate test of willingness to sacrifice his own son if that was required.

Two final features of the human self provide a fitting transition to our final theological doctrine, the Day of Judgment, for it is there that they come into sharpest relief. The two are the soul's individuality and its freedom.

To begin with the first of these: Coming to Islam, we are struck by the stress the Koran places on the self's individuality: its uniqueness and the responsibility that devolves on it alone. In India the all-pervading cosmic spirit comes close to swallowing the individual self, and in China the self is so ecological that where it begins and ends is hard to determine. Islam and its Semitic allies reverse this drift, regarding individuality as not only real but good in principle. Value, virtue, and spiritual fulfillment come through realizing the potentialities that are uniquely one's own; in ways that are not inconsequential, those possibilities differ from those of every other soul that ever has lived, or ever will live in the future. As an important Muslim philosopher has written, "This inexplicable finite centre of experience is the fundamental fact of the universe. All life is individual; there is no such thing as universal life. God Himself is an individual; He is the most unique individual."[5]

The individuality of the human soul is everlasting, for once it is created it never dies. Never, though, is its distinctness more acutely sensed than on the Day of Judgment. "O son of Adam, you will die alone, and enter the tomb alone, and be resurrected alone, and it is with you alone that the reckoning will be made" (Hasan al-Basri).

This reckoning and its correlate, responsibility, lead directly to the issue of the soul's freedom, and it must be admitted that in Islam human freedom stands in tension with God's omnipotence, which points toward predestination. Islamic theology has wrestled interminably with this tension without rationally resolving it. It concludes that the workings of the Divine Decree remain a mystery to humans, who nevertheless are granted sufficient freedom and responsibility to make genuine moral and spiritual decisions. "Whoever gets to himself a sin, gets it solely on his own responsibility . . . Whoever goes astray, he himself bears the whole responsibility of wandering" (4:111, 10:103).

As for the issue of judgment itself, Muslims consider it to be one of the illusions of modernity that we can, as it were, slip quietly away and not be noticed so long as we live (according to our own opinion) decent and harmless lives and do not draw attention to ourselves. It is the tearing away of all such illusions of security that characterizes the doctrine of the Last Judgment and its anticipation in the Koran. "When the sun shall be folded up, and the stars shall fall, and when the mountains shall be set in motion . . . and the seas shall boil. . . . Then shall every soul know what it has done" (81, *passim*). It is against this background that the Koran presents life as a brief but immensely precious opportunity, offering a once-and-for-all choice. Herein lies the urgency that informs the entire book. The chance to return to life for even a single day to make good use of their opportunities is something "the losers," facing their Reckoning, would treasure beyond anything they desired while they were still alive (14:14).

Depending on how it fares in its Reckoning, the soul will repair to either the heavens or the hells, which in the Koran are described in vivid, concrete, and sensual imagery. The masses of the faithful consider them to be actual places, which is perhaps the inevitable consequence of such depiction. In the heavens we are treated to fountains, cool shades, and chaste *houris* in gardens beneath which rivers flow; to carpets, cushions, goblets of gold, and sumptuous food and drink. In the hells there are burning garments, molten drinks, maces of iron, and fire that splits rocks into fragments. To say that these are nothing but symbols of the posthumous worlds—more rightly regarded as posthumous conditions of experience—is not to explain them away; but the object of the book is to present the hereafter in images of such vividness "that the hearts of those who do not believe in the Hereafter may incline to it" (6:113). The sharpness of the contrast between heaven and hell is intended to pull the hearer/reader of the Koran out of the spiritual lethargy that *ghaflah*, forgetfulness, induces.

The device works in periods of spiritual awareness and rebirth. In modern times it may be less effective for worldly-minded Muslims. In defense of allegorical interpretations of the images, liberal Muslims quote the Koran itself: "Some of the signs are firm—these are the basis of the book—and others are figurative" (3:5). Also supporting less materialistic views of paradise is Muhammad's statement that for the favored, "to see God's face night and morning [is] a felicity which will surpass all the pleasures of the body, as the ocean surpasses a drop of sweat."[6] Underlying the differences of interpretation, the belief that unites all Muslims concerning the afterlife is that each soul will be held accountable for its actions on earth with its future thereafter dependent upon how well it has observed God's commands. "We have hung every man's actions around his neck, and on the last day a wide-open book will be laid before him" (17:13).

As a final point: If all this talk of judgment still seems to cast God too much in the role of punisher, we can resort to verses in the Koran that remove Allah from direct involvement altogether. There souls judge themselves. What death burns away is self-serving defenses, forcing one to see with total objectivity how one has lived one's life. In the uncompromising light of that vision, where no dark and hidden corners are allowed, it is one's own actions that rise up to accuse or confirm. Once the self is extracted from the realm of lies, the falsities by which it armored itself become like flames, and the life it there led like a shirt of Nessus.

God, Creation, the Human Self, and the Day of Judgment—these are the chief theological pegs on which the Koran's teachings hang. In spite of their importance, however, the Koran is "a book which emphasizes deed rather than idea" (Muhammad Iqbal). It is to these deeds that we turn in the next two chapters.

— 6 —
THE
FIVE PILLARS

I f a Muslim were asked to summarize the way Islam counsels people to live, the answer might be: It teaches them to walk the straight path. The phrase comes from the opening *surah* of the Koran, which is repeated many times in the Muslim's five daily prayers.

> *In the Name of Allah the Merciful, the Compassionate:*
> *Praise be to Allah, Creator of the worlds,*
> *The Merciful, the Compassionate,*
> *Ruler of the day of Judgment.*
> *Thee do we worship, and Thee do we ask for aid.*
> *Guide us in the straight path,*
> *The path of those on whom Thou hast poured forth Thy*
> *   grace.*
> *Not the path of those who have incurred Thy wrath*
> *   and gone astray.*

This *surah* has been called the heartbeat of the Muslim's response to God. At the moment, though, the question is why "the straight path"? One meaning is obvious; a straight path is one that is not crooked or corrupt. The phrase contains another meaning, however, which addresses something that in Islam is distinctive. The straight path is one that is straightforward; it is direct and explicit. Compared with other religions, Islam spells out the way of life it proposes; it pinpoints it, nailing it down through clear injunctions. Every major type of action is classified on a sliding scale from the "forbidden," through the "indifferent," to the "obligatory." This gives the religion a flavor of definiteness that is quite its own. Muslims know where they stand.

They claim this as one of their religion's strengths. God's revelation to humankind, they say, has proceeded through four great stages. First, God revealed the truth of monotheism, God's oneness, through Abraham. Second, God revealed the Ten Commandments through Moses. Third, God revealed the Golden Rule—that we are to do unto others as we would have them do unto us—through Jesus. All three of these prophets were authentic messengers; each introduced important features of the God-directed life. One question yet remained, however: *How* should we love our neighbor? Once life became complicated, instructions were needed to answer that question, and the Koran provides them. "The glory of Islam consists in having embodied the beautiful sentiments of Jesus in definite laws."[1]

What, then, is the content of this straight path that spells out human duties? We shall divide our presentation into two parts. In this section we shall consider the Five Pillars of Islam, the principles that regulate the private life of Muslims in their dealings with God. In the next chapter we shall consider the Koran's social teachings.

The first of the Five Pillars is Islam's creed, or confession of faith known as the *Shahadah*. Every religion contains professions that orient its adherents' lives. Islam's wastes no words. Brief, simple, and explicit, it consists of a single sentence: "There is no god but God, and Muhammad is His Prophet." The first half of the proclamation announces the cardinal principle of monotheism. "There is no god but Allah." There is no god but *the* God. More directly still, there is no God but *God*, for the word is not a common noun embracing a class of objects; it is a proper name designating a unique being and him only. The second affirmation— that "Muhammad is God's prophet"—registers the Muslim's faith in the authenticity of Muhammad and in the validity of the book he transmitted.

At least once during his or her lifetime a Muslim must say the *Shahadah* correctly, slowly, thoughtfully, aloud, with full understanding and with heartfelt conviction. In actuality Muslims pronounce it often, especially its first half, *La ilaha illa 'llah*. In every crisis and at every moment when the world threatens to overwhelm them, not excepting the approach of death, "There is no god but God" will spring to their lips. "A pious man, seized by rage, will appear suddenly to have been stopped in his tracks as he remembers the *Shahadah* and, as it were, withdraws, putting a great distance between himself and his turbulent emotions. A woman crying out in childbirth will as suddenly fall silent, remembering; and a student, bowed anxiously over his desk in an examination hall, will raise his head and speak these words, and a barely audible sigh of relief passes through the whole assembly. This is the ultimate answer to all questions."[2]

The second pillar of Islam is the canonical prayer, in which the Koran adjures the faithful to "be constant" (29:45).

Muslims are admonished to be constant in prayer to keep their lives in perspective. The Koran considers this the most difficult lesson people must learn. Though they are obviously creatures, having created neither themselves nor their worlds, they can't seem to get this straight and keep placing themselves at the center of things, living as if they were laws unto themselves. This produces havoc. When we ask, then, why Muslims pray, a partial answer is: in response to life's natural impulse to give thanks for its existence. The deeper answer, however, is the one with which this paragraph opened: to keep life in perspective—to see it objectively, which involves acknowledging human creatureliness before its Creator. In practice this comes down to submitting one's will to God's *(islam)* as its rightful sovereign.

How often should Muslims pray? There is an account in the Koran that speaks to this point.

One of the crucial events in Muhammad's life, we are told, was his renowned Night Journey to Heaven. On a certain night in the month of Ramadan, he was spirited on a wondrous white steed with wings to Jerusalem and upward from there through the seven heavens to the presence of God, who instructed him that Muslims were to pray fifty times each day. On his way back to earth, he stopped in the sixth heaven, where he reported the instruction to Moses, who was incredulous. "Fifty times a day!" he said in effect. "You've got to be kidding. That will never work. Go back and negotiate." Muhammad did so and returned with the number reduced to forty, but Moses was not satisfied. "I know those people," he said. "Go back." This routine was repeated four more times, with the number reduced successively to thirty, twenty, ten, and then five. Even this last figure struck Moses as excessive. "Your people are not capable of observing five daily prayers," he said. "I have tested men before your time and have labored most earnestly to prevail over the [sons of] Isra'il, so go back to your Lord and ask Him to make things lighter for your people." This time, however, Muhammad refused. "I have asked my Lord till I am ashamed, but now I am satisfied and I submit." The number remained fixed at five.[3]

The times of the five prayers are likewise stipulated: on arising, when the sun reaches its zenith, its mid-decline, sunset, and before retiring. The schedule is not absolutely binding. The Koran says explicitly, for example, that "When you journey about the earth it is no crime that you come short in prayer if you fear that those who disbelieve will attack you." Under normal conditions, however, the fivefold pattern should be maintained. While in Islam no day of the week is as sharply set apart from the others as is the Sabbath for the Jews or Sunday for the Christians, Friday most nearly approximates a weekly holy day. Congregational worship is not stressed as much in Islam as it is in Judaism and Christianity; even so, Muslims are expected to pray in mosques when they can, and the Friday noon prayer is emphasized in this respect. Visitors to Muslim lands testify that one of the impressive religious sights in the world comes to view when, in a dimly lighted mosque, hundreds of Muslims stand shoulder to shoulder, then repeatedly kneel and prostrate themselves toward Mecca.

Although Muslims first prayed in the direction of Jerusalem, a koranic revelation later instructed them to pray in the direction of Mecca; and the realization that Muslims throughout the world do this creates a sense of participating in a worldwide fellowship, even when one prays in solitude. Beyond this matter of direction the Koran says almost nothing, but Muhammad's teachings and practices moved in to structure the void. Washing, to purify the body and symbolically the soul, precedes the prayer, which begins in dignified, upright posture but climaxes when the supplicant has sunk to his or her knees with forehead touching the floor. This is the prayer's holiest moment, for it carries a twofold symbolism. On the one hand, the body is in a fetal position, ready to be reborn. At the same time it is crouched in the smallest possible space, signifying human nothingness in the face of the divine.

As for prayer's content, its standard themes are praise, gratitude, and supplication. There is a Muslim saying that every time a bird drinks a drop of water it lifts its eyes in gratitude toward heaven. At least five times each day, Muslims do likewise.

The third pillar of Islam is charity. Material things are important in life, but some people have more than others. Why? Islam is not concerned with this theoretical question. Instead, it turns to the practical issue of what should be done about the disparity. Its answer is simple. Those who have much should help lift the burden of those who are less fortunate. It is a principle that twentieth-century democracies have embraced in secular mode in their concept of the welfare state. The Koran introduced its basic principle in the seventh century by prescribing a graduated tax on the haves to relieve the circumstances of the have-nots.

Details aside, the figure the Koran set for this tax was $2\frac{1}{2}$ percent. Alongside the tithe of Judaism and Christianity (which, being directed more to the maintenance of religious institutions than to the direct relief of human need, is not strictly comparable), this looks modest until we discover that it refers not just to income but to holdings. Poorer people owe nothing, but those in the middle and upper income brackets should annually distribute among the poor one-fortieth of the value of all they possess.

And to whom among the poor should this money be given? This too is prescribed: to those in immediate need; to slaves in the process of buying their freedom; to debtors unable to meet their obligations; to strangers and wayfarers; and to those who collect and distribute the alms.

The fourth pillar of Islam is the observance of Ramadan. Ramadan is a month in the Islamic calendar—Islam's holy month, because during it Muhammad received his initial revelation and (ten years later) made his historic *Hijrah* (migration) from Mecca to Medina. To commemorate these two great occasions, able-bodied Muslims (who are not ill or involved in crises like war or unavoidable journeys) fast during

Ramadan. From the first moment of dawn to the setting of the sun, neither food nor drink nor smoke passes their lips; after sundown they may partake in moderation. As the Muslim calendar is lunar, Ramadan rotates around the year. When it falls in the winter its demands are not excessive. When, on the other hand, it falls during the scorching heat of the summer, to remain active during the long days without so much as a drop of water is an ordeal.

Why, then, does the Koran require it? For one thing, fasting makes one think, as every Jew who has observed the fast of Yom Kippur will attest. For another thing, fasting teaches self-discipline; one who can endure its demands will have less difficulty controlling the demands of appetites at other times. Fasting underscores the creature's dependence on God. Human beings, it is said, are as frail as rose petals; nevertheless, they assume airs and pretensions. Fasting calls one back to one's frailty and dependence. Finally, fasting sensitizes compassion. Only those who have been hungry can know what hunger means. People who have fasted for twenty-nine days within the year will be apt to listen more carefully when next approached by someone who is hungry.

Islam's fifth pillar is pilgrimage. Once during his or her lifetime every Muslim who is physically and economically in a position to do so is expected to journey to Mecca, where God's climactic revelation was first disclosed. The basic purpose of the pilgrimage is to heighten the pilgrim's devotion to God and his revealed will, but the practice has fringe benefits as well. It is, for example, a reminder of human equality. Upon reaching Mecca, pilgrims remove their normal attire, which carries marks of social status, and don two simple sheet-like garments. Thus everyone, on approaching Islam's earthly focus, wears the same thing. Distinctions of rank and hierarchy are removed, and prince and pauper stand before God in their undivided humanity. Pilgrimage also provides a useful service in international relations. It brings together people from various countries, demonstrating thereby that they share a loyalty that transcends loyalty to their nations and ethnic groupings. Pilgrims pick up information about other lands and peoples, and return to their homes with better understanding of one another.

The Five Pillars of Islam consist of things Muslims do to keep the house of Islam erect. There are also things they should not do. Gambling, thieving, lying, eating pork, drinking intoxicants, and being sexually promiscuous are some of these. Even Muslims who transgress these rulings acknowledge their acts as transgressions.

With the exception of charity, the precepts we have considered in this chapter pertain to the Muslim's personal life. We turn now to the social teachings of Islam.

SOCIAL TEACHINGS

"O men! listen to my words and take them to heart! Know ye that every Muslim is a brother to every other Muslim, and that you are now one brotherhood." These notable words, spoken by the Prophet during his "farewell pilgrimage" to Mecca shortly before his death, epitomize one of Islam's loftiest ideals and strongest emphases. The intrusion of nationalism in the last two centuries has played havoc with this ideal on the political level, but on the communal level it has remained discernibly intact. "There is something in the religious culture of Islam which inspired, in even the humblest peasant or peddler, a dignity and a courtesy toward others never exceeded and rarely equalled in other civilizations," a leading Islamicist has written.[1]

Looking at the difference between pre- and post-Islamic Arabia, we are forced to ask whether history has ever witnessed a comparable moral advance among so many people in so short a time. Before Muhammad there was virtually no restraint on inter-tribal violence. Glaring inequities in wealth and possession were accepted as the natural order of things. Women were regarded more as possessions than as human beings. Rather than say that a man could marry an unlimited number of wives, it would be more accurate to say that his relations with women were so casual that beyond the first wife or two they scarcely approximated marriage at all. Infanticide was common, especially of girls. Drunkenness and large-scale gambling have already been remarked upon. Within a half-century there was effected a remarkable change in the moral climate on all of these counts.

Something that helped it to accomplish this near-miracle is a feature of Islam that we have already alluded to, namely its explicitness. Its basic objective in interpersonal relations, Muslims will say, is precisely that of Jesus and the other prophets: brotherly and sisterly love. The distinctive thing about Islam is not its ideal but the detailed prescriptions it sets forth for achieving it. We have already encountered its theory on this point. If Jesus had had a longer career, or if the Jews had not been so socially powerless at the time, Jesus might have systematized his teachings more. As it was, his work "was left unfinished. It was reserved for another Teacher to systematize the laws of morality."[2]

The Koran is this later teacher. In addition to being a spiritual guide, it is a legal compendium. When its innumerable prescriptions are supplemented by the only slightly less authoritative *hadith*—traditions based on what Muhammad did or said on his own initiative— we are not surprised to find Islam the most socially explicit of the Semitic religions. Westerners who define religion in terms of personal experience would never be understood by Muslims, whose religion calls them to establish a specific kind of social order. Islam joins faith to politics, religion to society, inseparably.

Islamic law is of enormous scope. It will be enough for our purposes if we summarize its provisions in four areas of collective life.

Economics

Islam is acutely aware of the physical foundations of life. Until bodily needs are met, higher concerns cannot flower. When one of Muhammad's followers ran up to him crying, "My Mother is dead; what is the best alms I can give away for the good of her soul?" the Prophet, thinking of the heat of the desert, answered instantly, "Water! Dig a well for her, and give water to the thirsty."

Just as the health of an organism requires that nourishment be fed to its every segment, so too a society's health requires that material goods be widely and appropriately distributed. These are the basic principles of Islamic economics, and nowhere do Islam's democratic impulses speak with greater force and clarity. The Koran, supplemented by *hadith*, propounded measures that broke the barriers of economic caste and enormously reduced the injustices of special interest groups.

The model that animates Muslim economics is the body's circulatory system. Health requires that blood flow freely and vigorously; sluggishness can bring on illness, blood clots occasion death. It is not different with the body politic, in which wealth takes the place of blood as the life-giving substance. As long as this analogy is honored and laws are in place to ensure that wealth is in vigorous circulation, Islam does not object to the profit motive, economic competition, or entrepreneurial ventures—the more imaginative the latter, the better. So freely are these allowed that some have gone so far as to characterize the Koran as "a businessman's book." It does not discourage people from working harder than their neighbors, nor object to such people being rewarded with larger returns. It simply insists that acquisitiveness and competition be balanced by the fair play that "keeps arteries open," and by compassion that is strong enough to pump life-giving blood—material resources—into the circulatory system's smallest capillaries. These "capillaries" are fed by the Poor Due, which (as has been noted) stipulates that annually a portion of one's holdings be distributed to the poor.

As for the way to prevent "clotting," the Koran went after the severest economic curse of the day—primogeniture—and flatly outlawed it. By restricting inheritance to the oldest son, this institution had concentrated wealth in a limited number of enormous estates. In banning the practice, the Koran sees to it that inheritance is shared by all heirs, daughters as well as sons. F. S. C. Northrop describes the settlement of a Muslim's estate that he chanced to witness. The application of Islamic law that afternoon resulted in the division of some $53,000 among no less than seventy heirs.

One verse in the Koran prohibits the taking of interest. At the time this was not only humane but eminently just, for loans were used then to tide the unfortunate over in times of disaster. With the rise of capitalism, however, money has taken on a new meaning. It now functions importantly as venture capital, and in this setting borrowed money multiplies. This benefits the borrower, and it is patently unjust to exclude the lender from his or her gain. The way Muslims have accommodated to this change is by making lenders in some way partners in the venture for which their monies are used. When capitalism is approached in this manner, Muslims find no incompatibility between its central feature, venture capital, and Islam. Capitalism's excesses—which Muslims consider to be glaringly exhibited in the secular West—are another matter. The equalizing provisos of the Koran would, if duly applied, offset them.

The Status of Women

Chiefly because it permits a plurality of wives, Islam has been accused by the West of degrading women.

If we approach the issue of women's status historically, comparing the status of Arabian women before and after Muhammad, the charge is patently false. In the pre-Islamic "days of ignorance," marriage arrangements were so loose as to be scarcely recognizable. Women were regarded as little more than chattel, to be done with as fathers or husbands pleased. Daughters had no inheritance rights and were often buried alive in their infancy.

Addressing conditions in which the very birth of a daughter was regarded as a calamity, the koranic reforms improved woman's status incalculably They forbade infanticide. They required that daughters be included in inheritance—not equally, it is true, but to half the proportion of sons, which seems just, in view of the fact that unlike sons, daughters would not assume financial responsibility for their households. In her rights as citizen—education, suffrage, and vocation—the Koran leaves open the possibility of woman's full equality with man, an equality that is being approximated as the customs of Muslim nations become modernized.³ If in another century women under Islam do not attain the social position of their Western sisters, a position to which the latter have been brought by industrialism and democracy rather than religion, it will then be time, Muslims say, to hold Islam accountable.

It was in the institution of marriage, however, that Islam made its greatest contribution to women. Muslims consider the family the foundation of a good society and marriage its cornerstone. Women—as daughters, wives, and especially mothers—are to be treated with utmost love and respect. Islam sanctified marriage, first and primarily, by making it the sole lawful locus of the sexual act.⁴

To the adherents of a religion in which the punishment for adultery is death by stoning and social dancing is proscribed, Western indictments of Islam as a lascivious religion sound ill-directed. Second, the Koran requires that a woman give her free consent before she may be wed; not even a sultan may marry without his bride's express approval. Third, Islam tightened the wedding bond enormously. Though Muhammad did not forbid divorce, he countenanced it only as a last resort. Asserting repeatedly that nothing displeased God more than the disruption of marital vows, he instituted legal provisions to keep marriages intact. At the time of marriage husbands are required to provide the wife with a sum on which both agree and which she retains in its entirety should a divorce ensue. Divorce proceedings call for three distinct and separate periods, in each of which arbiters drawn from both families try to reconcile the two parties. Though such devices are intended to keep divorces to a minimum, wives no less than husbands are permitted to instigate them.

There remains, however, the issue of polygamy, or more precisely polygyny. It is true that the Koran permits a man to have up to four wives simultaneously, but there is a growing consensus that a careful reading of its regulations on the matter point toward monogamy as the ideal. Supporting this view is the Koran's statement that "if you cannot deal equitably and justly with [more than one wife], you shall marry only one." Other passages make it clear that "equality" here refers not only to material perquisites but to love and esteem. In physical arrangements each wife must have private quarters, and this in itself is a limiting factor. It is the second proviso, though—equality of love and esteem—that leads jurists to argue that the Koran virtually enjoins monogamy, for it is almost impossible to distribute affection and regard with exact equality. This interpretation has been in the Muslim picture since the third century of the *Hijrah*, and it is gaining increasing acceptance. To avoid any possible misun-

derstanding, many Muslims now insert in the marriage deed a clause by which the husband formally
renounces his supposed right to a second concurrent
spouse, and in point of fact—with the exception of
African tribes where polygyny is customary—multiple wives are seldom found in Islam today.

Nevertheless, the fact remains that the Koran does
permit polygyny: "You may marry two, three, or four
wives, but not more." And what are we to make of
Muhammad's own multiple marriages? Muslims take
both items as instances of Islam's versatility in addressing diverse circumstances.

There are circumstances in the imperfect condition
we know as human existence when polygyny is morally
preferable to its alternative. Individually, such a condition might arise if, early in marriage, the wife were to
contract paralysis or another disability that would prevent sexual union. Collectively, a war that decimated the
male population could provide an example, forcing (as
this would) the option between polygyny and depriving
a large proportion of women of motherhood and a
nuclear family of any sort. Idealists may call for the exer-
cise of heroic continence in such circumstances, but
heroism is never a mass option. The actual choice is
between a legalized polygyny in which sex is tightly
joined to responsibility, and alternatively monogamy,
which, being unrealistic, fosters prostitution, where men
disclaim responsibility for their sexual partners and

their progeny. Pressing their case, Muslims point out that multiple marriages are at least as common in the West; the difference is that they are successive. Is "serial polygyny," the Western version, self-evidently superior to its coeval form, when women have the right to opt out of the arrangement (through divorce) if they want to? Finally, Muslims, though they have spoken frankly from the first of female sexual fulfillment as a marital right, do not skirt the volatile question of whether the male sexual drive is stronger than the female's. "Hoggledy higamous, men are polygamous; /Higgledy hogamus, women monogamous," Dorothy Parker wrote flippantly. If there is biological truth in her limerick, "rather than allowing this sensuality in the male to run riot, obeying nothing but its own impulses, the Law of Islam sets down a polygynous framework that provides a modicum of control. [It] confers a conscious mold on the formless instinct of man in order to keep him within the structures of religion."[5]

As for the veiling of women and their seclusion generally, the koranic injunction is restrained. It says only to "Tell your wives and your daughters and the women of the believers to draw their cloaks closely round them (when they go abroad). That will be better, so that they may be recognised and not annoyed" (33:59). Extremes that have evolved from this ruling are matters of local custom and are not religiously binding.

Somewhere in this chapter on social issues the subject of penalties should be mentioned, for the impression is widespread that Islamic law imposes ones that are excessively harsh. This is a reasonable place to address this issue, for one of the most frequently cited examples is the punishment for adultery, which repeats the Jewish law of death by stoning—two others that are typically mentioned are severance of the thief's hand, and flogging for a number of offenses. These stipulations are indeed severe, but (as Muslims see matters) this is to make the point that the injuries that occasion these penalties are likewise severe and will not be tolerated. Once this juridical point is in place, mercy moves in to temper the decrees. "Avert penalties by doubt," Muhammad told his people, and Islamic jurisprudence legitimizes any stratagem that averts the penalty without outright impugning the Law. Stoning for adultery is made almost impossible by the proviso that four unimpeachable witnesses must have observed the act in detail. "Flogging" can be technically fulfilled by using a light sandal or even the hem of a garment, and thieves may retain their hands if the theft was from genuine need.

Race Relations

Islam stresses racial equality and "has achieved a remarkable degree of interracial coexistence."[6] The ultimate test in this area is willingness to intermarry, and Muslims see Abraham as modeling this willingness in marrying Hagar, a black woman whom they regard as his second wife rather than a concubine. Under Elijah Muhammad the Black Muslim movement in America—it has had various names—was militant toward the whites; but when Malcolm X made his 1964 pilgrimage to Mecca, he discovered that racism had no precedent in Islam and could not be accommodated to it.[7] Muslims like to recall that the first *muezzin*, Bilal, was an Ethiopian who prayed regularly for the conversion of the Koreish—"whites" who were persecuting the early believers, many of whom were black. The advances that Islam continues to make in Africa is not unrelated to this religion's principled record on this issue.

The Use of Force

Muslims report that the standard Western stereotype that they encounter is that of a man marching with sword outstretched, followed by a long train of wives. Not surprisingly, inasmuch as from the beginning (a historian reports) Christians have believed that "the two most important aspects of Muhammad's life . . . are his sexual licence and his use of force to establish religion."[8] Muslims feel that both Muhammad and the

Koran have been maligned on these counts. License was discussed above. Here we turn to force.

Admit, they say, that the Koran does not counsel turning the other cheek, or pacifism. It teaches forgiveness and the return of good for evil when the circumstances warrant—"turn away evil with that which is better" (42:37)—but this is different from not resisting evil. Far from requiring the Muslim to turn himself into a doormat for the ruthless, the Koran allows punishment of wanton wrongdoers to the full extent of the injury they impart (22:39–40). Justice requires this, they believe; abrogate reciprocity, which the principle of fair play requires, and morality descends to impractical idealism if not sheer sentimentality. Extend this principle of justice to collective life and we have as one instance *jihad*, the Muslim concept of a holy war, in which the martyrs who die are assured of heaven. All this the Muslim will affirm as integral to Islam, but we are still a far cry from the familiar charge that Islam spread primarily by the sword and was upheld by the sword.

As an outstanding general, Muhammad left many traditions regarding the decent conduct of war. Agreements are to be honored and treachery avoided; the wounded are not to be mutilated, nor the dead disfigured. Women, children, and the old are to be spared, as are orchards, crops, and sacred objects. These, however, are not the point. The important question is the definition of a righteous war. According to prevailing interpretations of the Koran, a righteous war must either be defensive or to right a wrong. "Defend yourself against your enemies, but do not attack them first: God hates the aggressor" (2:190). The aggressive and unrelenting hostility of the idolaters forced Muhammad to seize the sword in self-defense, or, together with his entire community and his God-entrusted faith, be wiped from the face of the earth. That other teachers succumbed under force and became martyrs was to Muhammad no reason that he should do the same. Having seized the sword in self-defense he held on to it to the end. This much Muslims acknowledge; but they insist that while Islam has at times spread by the sword, it has mostly spread by persuasion and example.

The crucial verses in the Koran bearing on conversion read as follows:

Let there be no compulsion in religion.
(2:257)

To every one have We given a law and a way. . . . And if God had pleased, he would have made [all humankind] one people [people of one religion]. But he hath done otherwise, that He might try you in that which He hath severally given unto you: wherefore press forward in good

works. Unto God shall ye return, and He will tell you
that concerning which ye disagree.

(5:48)

Muslims point out that Muhammad incorporated
into his charter for Medina the principle of religious
toleration that these verses announce. They regard that
document as the first charter of freedom of conscience
in human history and the authoritative model for
those of every subsequent Muslim state. It decreed
that "the Jews who attach themselves to our commonwealth [similar rights were later mentioned for
Christians, these two being the only non-Muslim religions on the scene] shall be protected from all insults
and vexations; they shall have an equal right with our
own people to our assistance and good offices: the
Jews . . . and all others domiciled in Yathrib, shall . . .
practice their religion as freely as the Muslims." Even
conquered nations were permitted freedom of worship contingent only on the payment of a special tax in
lieu of the Poor Due, from which they were exempt;
thereafter every interference with their liberty of conscience was regarded as a direct contravention of
Islamic law. If clearer indication than this of Islam's
stand on religious tolerance be asked, we have the
direct words of Muhammad: "Will you then force men
to believe when belief can come only from God?"[9]

Once, when a deputy of Christians visited him, Muhammad invited them to conduct their service in his mosque, adding, "It is a place consecrated to God."

This much for theory and Muhammad's personal example. How well Muslims have lived up to his principles of toleration is a question of history that is far too complex to admit of a simple, objective, and definitive answer. On the positive side Muslims point to the long centuries during which, in India, Spain, and the Near East, Christians, Jews, and Hindus lived quietly and in freedom under Muslim rule. Even under the worst rulers Christians and Jews held positions of influence and in general retained their religious freedom. It was Christians, not Muslims, we are reminded, who in the fifteenth century expelled the Jews from Spain where, under Islamic rule, they had enjoyed one of their golden ages. To press this example, Spain and Anatolia changed hands at about the same time—Christians expelled the Moors from Spain, while Muslims conquered what is now Turkey. Every Muslim was driven from Spain, put to the sword, or forced to convert, whereas the seat of the Eastern Orthodox church remains in Istanbul to this day. Indeed, if comparisons are what we want, Muslims consider Christianity's record as the darker of the two. Who was it, they ask, who preached the Crusades in the name of the Prince of Peace? Who instituted the Inquisition, invented the rack and the stake as instruments of religion, and plunged Europe into its devastating wars of religion? Objective historians are of one mind in their verdict that, to put the matter minimally, Islam's record on the use of force is no darker than that of Christianity.

Laying aside comparisons, Muslims admit that their own record respecting force is not exemplary. Every religion at some stages in its career has been used by its professed adherents to mask aggression, and Islam is no exception. Time and again it has provided designing chieftains, caliphs, and now heads of state with pretexts for gratifying their ambitions. What Muslims deny can be summarized in three points.

First, they deny that Islam's record of intolerance and aggression is greater than that of the other major religions. (Buddhism may be an exception here.)

Second, they deny that Western histories are fair to Islam in their accounts of its use of force.[10] *Jihad,* they say, is a case in point. To Westerners it conjures scenes of screaming fanatics being egged into war by promises that they will be instantly transported to heaven if they are slain. In actuality: (a) *jihad* literally means exertion, though because war requires exertion in exceptional degree the word is often, by extension, attached thereto. (b) The definition of a holy war in Islam is virtually identical with that of a just war in Christianity, where too it is sometimes called a holy war. (c) Christianity, too, considers those who die in

such wars to be martyrs, and promises them salvation.
(d) A *hadith* (canonical saying) of Muhammad ranks
the battle against evil within one's own heart above
battles against external enemies. "We have returned
from the lesser *jihad*," the Prophet observed, following
an encounter with the Meccans, "to face the greater
jihad," the battle with the enemy within oneself.

For he believed, as most Muslims believe today,
that the essential hiahd is the spiritual struggle of the
soul to ascend to unity with God. External warfare is to
be only a temporary defensive measure to assure the
safety to live a good life in surrender to God.

Third, Muslims deny that the blots in their record
should be charged against their religion whose presiding ideal they affirm in their standard greeting,
as-salamu 'alaykum ("Peace be upon you").

— 8 —

SUFISM

We have been treating Islam as if it were mono-
lithic, which of course it is not. Like every religious tradition it divides. Its main historical division is
between the mainstream Sunnis ("Traditionalists"
[from *sunnah*, tradition] who comprise 87 percent of
all Muslims) and the Shi'ites (literally "partisans" of
Ali, Muhammad's son-in-law, whom Shi'ites believe
should have directly succeeded Muhammad but who
was thrice passed over and who, when he was finally
appointed leader of the Muslims, was assassinated).
Geographically, the Shi'ites cluster in and around Iraq
and Iran, while the Sunnis flank them to the West (the
Middle East, Turkey, and Africa) and to the East
(through the Indian subcontinent, which includes
Pakistan and Bangladesh, on through Malaysia, and
into Indonesia, where alone there are more Muslims
than in the entire Arab world). We shall pass over this

historical split, which turns on an in-house dispute, and take up instead a division that has universal overtones. It is the vertical division between the mystics of Islam, called Sufis, and the remaining majority of the faith, who are equally good Muslims but are not mystics.

The root meaning of the word Sufi is wool, *suf.* A century or two after Muhammad's death, those within the Islamic community who bore the inner message of Islam came to be known as Sufis. Many of them donned coarse woolen garments to protest the silks and satins of sultans and califs. Alarmed by the worldliness they saw overtaking Islam, they sought to purify and spiritualize it from within. They wanted to recover its liberty and love, and to restore to it its deeper, mystical tone. Externals should yield to internals, matter to meaning, outward symbol to inner reality. "Love the pitcher less," they cried, "and the water more."

Sufis saw this distinction between the inner and the outer, the pitcher and what it contains, as deriving from the Koran itself, where Allah presents himself as both "the Outward *[al-zahir]* and the Inward *[al-batin]*" (57:3). Exoteric Muslims—we shall call them such because they were satisfied with the explicit meanings of the Koran's teachings—passed over this distinction, but the Sufis (esoteric Muslims) found it important. Contemplation of God occupies a significant place in every Muslim's life, but for most it must compete, pretty much on a par, with life's other demands. When we add to this that life is demanding—people tend to be busy—it stands to reason that not many Muslims will have the time, if the inclination, to do more than keep up with the Divine Law that orders their lives. Their fidelity is not in vain; in the end their reward will be as great as the Sufis'. But the Sufis were impatient for their reward, if we may put the matter thus. They wanted to encounter God directly in this very lifetime. Now.

This called for special methods, and to develop and practice them the Sufis gathered around spiritual masters (shaikhs), forming circles that, from the twelfth century onward, crystallized into Sufi orders *(tariqahs)*. The word for the members of these orders is *faqir*—pronounced *fakir*; literally poor, but with the connotation of one who is "poor in spirit." In some ways, however, they constituted a spiritual elite, aspiring higher than other Muslims, and willing to assume the heavier disciplines their extravagant goals required. We can liken their *tariqahs* to the contemplative orders of Roman Catholicism, with the difference that Sufis generally marry and are not cloistered. They engage in normal occupations and repair to their gathering places (*zawiyahs*, Arabic; *khanaqahs*, Persian) to sing, dance, pray, recite their rosaries in concert, and listen to the discourses of their Master, all to the end of reaching God directly. Someone who was ignorant of fire, they observe, could come to know it by degrees:

first by hearing of it, then by seeing it, and finally by being burned by its heat. The Sufis wanted to be "burned" by God.

This required drawing close to him, and they developed three overlapping but distinguishable routes. We can call these the mysticisms of love, of ecstasy, and of intuition.

To begin with the first of these, Sufi love poetry is world famous. A remarkable eighth-century woman saint, Rabi'a, discovered in her solitary vigils, often lasting all night, that God's love was at the core of the universe; not to steep oneself in that love and reflect it to others was to forfeit life's supreme beatitude. Because love is never more evident than when its object is absent, that being the time when the beloved's importance cannot be overlooked, Persian poets in particular dwelt on the pangs of separation to deepen their love of God and thereby draw close to him. Jalal ad-Din Rumi used the plaintive sound of the reed flute to typify this theme.

> Listen to the story told by the reed, of being separated.
> "Since I was cut from the reedbed, I have made this
>   crying sound.
> Anyone separated from someone he loves understands
>   what I say, anyone pulled from a source longs to go
>   back."

The lament of the flute, torn from its riverbank and symbol therefore for the soul's severance from the divine, threw the Sufis into states of agitation and bewilderment. Nothing created could assuage those states; but its beloved, Allah, is so sublime, so dissimilar, that human love for him is like the nightingale's for the rose, or the moth's for the flame. Even so, Rumi assures us, that human love is returned:

Never does the lover seek without being sought by his beloved.

When the lightning of love has shot into this *heart, know that there is love in* that *heart. . . .*

Mark well the text: "He loves them and they love Him."

(Koran, 5:59)

But the full truth has still not been grasped, for Allah loves his creatures *more* than they love him. "God saith: Whoso seeketh to approach Me one span, I approach him one cubit; and whoso seeketh to approach Me one cubit, I approach him two fathoms; and whoever walks towards Me, I run towards him."[1] Rabi'a celebrates the eventual meeting of the two souls, one finite, the other Infinite, in her famous night prayer:

My God and my Lord: eyes are at rest, the stars are setting, hushed are the movements of birds in their nests, of monsters in the deep. And you are the Just who knows no change, the Equity that does not swerve, the Everlasting that never passes away. The doors of kings are locked and guarded by their henchmen, but your door is open to those who call upon you. My Lord, each lover is now alone with his beloved. And I am alone with you.

We are calling the second Sufi approach to the divine presence ecstatic (literally, "to stand outside oneself") because it turns on experiences that differ, not just in degree but in kind, from usual ones. The presiding metaphor for ecstatic Sufis was the Prophet's Night journey through the seven heavens into the Divine Presence. What he perceived in those heavens no one can say, but we can be sure the visions were extraordinary—increasingly so with each level of ascent. Ecstatic Sufis do not claim that they come to see what Muhammad saw that night, but they move in his direction. At times the content of what they are experiencing engrosses them so completely that their states become trancelike because of their total abstraction from self. No attention remains for who they are, where they are, or what is happening to them. In psychological parlance they are "dissociated" from themselves, losing consciousness of the world as it is normally perceived. Journeying to meet such adepts, pilgrims reported finding themselves ignored—not out of discourtesy, but because literally they were not seen. Deliberate inducement of such states required practice; a pilgrim who sought out a revered ecstatic named Nuri reported finding him in such an intense state of concentration that not a hair of his body moved. "When I later asked him, 'From whom did you learn this deep concentration?' he replied, 'From a cat watching by a mouse hole. But its concentration is much more intense than mine.'"[2] Nevertheless, when the altered state arrives, it feels like a gift rather than an acquisition. The phrase that mystical theology uses, "infused grace," feels right here; for Sufis report that as their consciousness begins to change, it feels as if their wills were placed in abeyance and a superior will takes over.

Sufis honor their ecstatics, but in calling them "drunken" they serve notice that they must bring the substance of their visions back with them when they find themselves "sober" again. In plain language, transcendence must be made immanent; the God who is encountered apart from the world must also be encountered within it. This latter does not require ecstasy as its preliminary, and the direct route to cultivating it carries us to the third Sufi approach: the way of intuitive discernment.

Like the other two methods this one brings knowledge, but of a distinct sort. Love mysticism yields "heart knowledge," and ecstasy "visual or visionary knowledge," because extraterrestrial realities are seen; but intuitive mysticism brings "mental knowledge, which Sufis call *ma'rifah*, obtained through an organ of discernment called "the eye of the heart."[3] Because the realities attained through *ma'rifah* are immaterial, the eye of the heart is immaterial as well. It does not compete with the physical eye whose objects, the world's normal objects, remain fully in view. What it does is clothe those objects in celestial light. Or to reverse the metaphor: It recognizes the world's objects as garments that God dons to create a world. These garments become progressively more transparent as the eye of the heart gains strength. It would be false to say that the world is *God*—that would be pantheism. But to the eye of the heart, the world *is* God-in-disguise, God veiled.

The principal method the Sufis employed for penetrating the disguise is symbolism. In using visible objects to speak of invisible things, symbolism is the language of religion generally; it is to religion what numbers are to science. Mystics, however, employ it to exceptional degree; for instead of stopping with the first spiritual object a symbol points to, they use it as stepping stone to a more exalted object. This led al-Ghazali to define symbolism as "the science of the relation between multiple levels of reality." Every verse of the Koran, the Sufis say, conceals a minimum of seven hidden significations, and the number can sometimes reach to seventy.

To illustrate this point: For all Muslims removing one's shoes before stepping into a mosque is a mark of reverence; it signifies checking the clamoring world at the door and not admitting it into sacred precincts. The Sufi accepts this symbolism fully, but goes on to see in the act the additional meaning of removing everything that separates the soul from God. Or the act of asking forgiveness. All Muslims pray to be forgiven for specific transgressions, but when the Sufi pronounces the formula *astaghfiru'llah, I* ask forgiveness of God, he or she reads into the petition an added request: to be forgiven for his or her separate existence. This sounds strange, and indeed, exoteric Muslims find it incomprehensible. But the Sufis see it as an extension of Rabi'a's teaching that "Your existence is a sin with which no other can be compared." Because *ex*-istence is a standing *out* from something, which in this case is God, existence involves separation.

To avoid it Sufis developed their doctrine of *fana*—extinction—as the logical term of their quest. Not that their *consciousness* was to be extinguished. It was their *self*-consciousness—their consciousness of themselves as separate selves replete with their private personal agendas—that was to be ended. If the ending was complete, they argued, when they looked inside the dry shells of their now-emptied selves they would find nothing but God. A Christian mystic put this point by writing:

God, whose boundless love and joy
Are present everywhere;
He cannot come to visit you
Unless you are not there.

(Angelus Silesius)

Al-Hallaj's version was: "I saw my Lord with the eye of the Heart. I said: 'Who are you?' He answered: 'You.'"

As a final example of the Sufis' extravagant use of symbolism, we can note the way they tightened the creedal assertion "There is no god but God" to read, "There is *nothing* but God." To exoteric Muslims this again sounded silly, if not blasphemous: silly because there are obviously lots of things—tables and chairs—that are not God; blasphemous because the mystic reading seemed to deny God as Creator. But the Sufis' intent was to challenge the independence that people normally ascribe to things. Monotheism to them meant more than the theoretical point that there are not two Gods; that they considered obvious. Picking up on the existential meaning of theism—God is that to which we give (or should give) ourselves—they agreed that the initial meaning of "no god but God" is that we should give ourselves to nothing but God. But we do not catch the full significance of the phrase, they argued, until we see that we *do* give ourselves to other things when we let them occupy us as objects in their own right; objects that have the power to interest or repel us by being simply what they are. To think of light as caused by electricity—by electricity only and sufficiently, without asking where electricity comes from—is in principle to commit *shirk;* for because only God is self-sufficient, to consider other things as such is to liken them to God and thereby ascribe to him rivals.

Symbolism, though powerful, works somewhat abstractly, so the Sufis supplement it with *dhikr* (to remember), the practice of remembering Allah through repeating his Name. "There is a means of polishing all things whereby rust may be removed," a *hadith* asserts, adding: "That which polishes the heart is the invocation of Allah." Remembrance of God is at the same time a forgetting of self, so Sufis consider the repetition of Allah's Name the best way of directing their attention Godward. Whether they utter God's Name alone or with others, silently or aloud, accenting its first syllable sharply or prolonging its second syllable as long as breath allows, they try to fill every free moment of the day with its music. Eventually, this practice kneads the syllables into the subconscious mind, from which they bubble up with the spontaneity of a birdsong.

The foregoing paragraphs sketch what Sufism is at heart, but they do not explain why this chapter opened by associating it with a division within Islam. The answer is that Muslims are of two minds about Sufism. This is partly because Sufism is itself a mixed bag. By the principle that the higher attracts the lower, Sufi orders have at times attracted riffraff who are Sufis in little more than name. For example, certain mendicant orders of Sufism have used poverty as a discipline, but it is only a step from authentic Sufis of this stripe to beggars who do no more than claim to be Sufis. Politics too has at times intruded. Most recently, groups have arisen in the West that call themselves Sufis, while professing no allegiance whatsoever to Islamic orthodoxy.

It is not surprising that these aberrations raise eyebrows, but even authentic Sufism (as we have tried to describe it) is controversial. Why? It is because Sufis take certain liberties that exoteric Muslims cannot in conscience condone. Having seen the sky through the skylight of Islamic orthodoxy, Sufis become persuaded that there is more sky than the aperture allows. When Rumi asserted, "I am neither Muslim nor Christian, Jew nor Zoroastrian; I am neither of the earth nor of the heavens, I am neither body nor soul," we can understand the exoterics' fear that orthodoxy was being strained beyond permissible limits. Ibn Arabi's declaration was even more unsettling:

My heart has opened unto every form. It is a pasture for gazelles, a cloister for Christian monks, a temple for idols, the Ka'ba of the pilgrim, the tablets of the Torah and the book of the Koran. I practice the religion of Love; in whatsoever directions its caravans advance, the religion of Love shall be my religion and my faith.

As for Al-Hallaj's assertion that he was God,[4] no explanation from the Sufis to the effect that he was referring to the divine Essence that was within him could keep exoterics from hearing this as outright blasphemy.

Mysticism breaks through the boundaries that protect the faith of the typical believer. In doing so it moves into an unconfined region that, fulfilling though it is for some, carries dangers for those who are unqualified for its teachings. Without their literal meaning being denied, dogmas and prescriptions that the ordinary believer sees as absolute are interpreted allegorically, or used as points of reference that may eventually be transcended. Particularly shocking to some is the fact that the Sufi often claims, if only by implication, an authority derived directly from God and a knowledge given from above rather than learned in the schools.

Sufis have their rights, but—if we may venture the verdict of Islam as a whole—so have ordinary believers whose faith in unambiguous principles, fully adequate for salvation, could be undermined by teachings that seem to tamper with them. For this reason many spiritual Masters have been discreet in their teachings, reserving parts of their doctrine for those who are suited to receive them. This is also why the exoteric authorities have regarded Sufism with understandable suspicion. Control has been exercised, partly by public opinion and partly by means of a kind of dynamic tension, maintained through the centuries, between the exoteric religious authorities on the one hand and Sufi *shaikhs* on the other. An undercurrent of opposition to Sufism within sections of the Islamic community has served as a necessary curb on the mystics, without this undercurrent having been strong enough to prevent those who have had a genuine vocation for a Sufi path from following their destiny.

On the whole, esoterism and exoterism have achieved a healthy balance in Islam, but in this chapter we shall let the esoterics have the last word. One of the teaching devices for which they are famous has not yet been mentioned; it is the Sufi tale. This one, "The Tale of the Sands," relates to their doctrine of *fana,* the transcending, in God, of the finite self.

A stream, from its source in far-off mountains, passing through every kind and description of countryside, at last reached the sands of the desert. Just as it had crossed every other barrier, the stream tried to cross this one, but it found that as fast as it ran into the sand, its waters disappeared.

It was convinced, however, that its destiny was to cross this desert, and yet there was no way. Now a hidden voice, coming from the desert itself, whispered: "The Wind crosses the desert, and so can the stream."

The stream objected that it was dashing itself against the sand, and only getting absorbed: that the wind could fly, and this was why it could cross a desert.

"By hurtling in your own accustomed way you cannot get across. You will either disappear or become a marsh. You must allow the wind to carry you over, to your destination."

But how could this happen? "By allowing yourself to be absorbed in the wind."

This idea was not acceptable to the stream. After all, it had never been absorbed before. It did not want to lose its individuality. And, once having lost it, how was one to know that it could ever be regained?

"The wind," said the sand, "performs this function. It takes up water, carries it over the desert, and then lets it fall again. Falling as rain, the water again becomes a river."

"How can I know that this is true?" "It is so, and if you do not believe it, you cannot become more than a quagmire, and even that could take many, many years. And it certainly is not the same as a stream."

"*But can I not remain the same stream that I am today?*"

"*You cannot in either case remain so,*" *the whisper said.* "*Your essential part is carried away and forms a stream again. You are called what you are even today because you do not know which part of you is the essential one.*"

When it heard this, certain echoes began to arise in the thoughts of the stream. Dimly it remembered a state in which it—or some part of it?—had been held in the arms of a wind. It also remembered—or did it?—that this was the real thing, not necessarily the obvious thing, to do.

And the stream raised its vapor into the welcoming arms of the wind, which gently and easily bore it upwards and along, letting it fall softly as soon as they reached the roof of a mountain, many, many, miles away. And because it had its doubts, the stream was able to remember and record more strongly in its mind the details of the experience. It reflected, "*Yes, now I have learned my true identity.*"

The stream was learning. But the sands whispered: "*We know, because we see it happen day after day: and because we, the sands, extend from the riverside all the way to the mountain.*"

And that is why it is said that the way in which the stream of Life is to continue on its journey is written in the Sands.[5]

WHITHER ISLAM?

For long periods since Muhammad called his people to God's oneness, Muslims have wandered from the spirit of the Prophet. Their leaders are the first to admit that practice has often been replaced by mere profession, and that fervor has waned.

Viewed as a whole, however, Islam unrolls before us one of the most remarkable panoramas in all history. We have spoken of its early greatness. Had we pursued its history there would have been chapters on the Muslim empire, which, a century after Muhammad's death, stretched from the bay of Biscay to the Indus and the frontiers of China, from the Aral Sea to the upper Nile. More important would have been the chapters describing the spread of Muslim ideas: the development of a fabulous culture, the rise of literature, science, medicine, art, and architecture; the glory of Damascus, Baghdad, and Egypt, and the splendor of Spain under the Moors. There would have been the story of how, during Europe's Dark Ages, Muslim philosophers and scientists kept the lamp of learning bright, ready to spark the Western mind when it roused from its long sleep.

Nor would the story have been entirely confined to the past, for there are indications that Islam is emerging from several centuries of stagnation, which colonization no doubt exacerbated. It faces enormous problems: how to distinguish industrial modernization (which on balance it welcomes), from Westernization (which on balance it doesn't); how to realize the unity that is latent in Islam when the forces of nationalism work powerfully against it; how to hold on to Truth in a pluralistic, relativizing age. But having thrown off the colonial yoke, Islam is stirring with some of the vigor of its former youth. From Morocco across from Gibraltar on the Atlantic, eastward across North Africa, through the Indian subcontinent (which includes Pakistan and Bangladesh), on to the near-tip of Indonesia, Islam is a vital force in the contemporary world. It numbers in the order of 1.2 billion, of which the vast majority are moderates and not radical fundamentalists. Read these words at any hour of day or night and somewhere from a minaret (or now by radio) a *muezzin* will be calling the faithful to prayer, announcing:

God is most great.
God is most great.
I testify that there is no god but God.
I testify that Muhammad is the Prophet of God.
Arise and pray;
God is most great.
God is most great.
There is no god but God.

SUGGESTIONS FOR
FURTHER READING

G ranting the Muslim's contention that the Koran suffers incomparably in translation, Mohammed Pickthall's *The Meaning of the Glorious Koran* (New York: New American Library, 1953) may be recommended as being as serviceable as any.

Kenneth Cragg's *The House of Islam* (Belmont, CA: Wadsworth, 1988) and Victor Danner's *The Islamic Tradition* (Amity, NY: Amity House, 1988) offer admirable overviews of this tradition, as do Seyyed Hossein Nasr's *Ideals and Realities of Islam* (San Francisco: HarperSanFrancisco, 1989) and Abdel Halim Mahmud's *The Creed of Islam* (London: World of Islam Festival Trust, 1978; distributed by Thorsons Publishers, Denington Estate, Wellingborough, Northants, England).

The best metaphysical discussion of Sufi doctrines is to be found in Frithjof Schuon's *Understanding Islam*

(New York: Penguin Books, 1972), which a leading Muslim scholar has hailed as "the best work in English on the meaning of Islam and why Muslims believe in it." It is a demanding book, however. More accessible to the general reader are William Stoddart's *Sufism* (New York: Paragon Press, 1986) and Martin Lings's *What Is Sufism?* (London: Unwin Hyman, 1975, 1988).

For the writings of the greatest Sufi poet, Rumi, Coleman Barks's *The Essential Rumi* (San Francisco: HarperSanFrancisco, 1995) and *The Soul of Rumi* (San Francisco: HarperSanFrancisco, 2001) are especially recommended.

My thirty-minute video cassette on "Islamic Mysticism: The Sufi Way" is available from Hartley Film Foundation, Cat Rock Road, Cos Cob, CT 06807.

The pleasures of Sufi tales can be sampled through Idries Shah's collection, *Tales of the Dervishes* (New York: E. P. Dutton, 1970).

NOTES

PROLOGUE

1. Meg Greenfield, *Newsweek* (March 26, 1979): 116.

2. Norman Daniel, *Islam and the West: The Making of an Image*, 1960. Rev. ed. (Edinburgh: Edinburgh University Press, 1966) details the emergence of the distorted picture of Islam that has dominated the West for over a thousand years.

ISLAMIC BACKGROUND

1. Philip Hitti, *History of the Arabs*, 1937. Rev. ed. (New York: St. Martin's Press, 1970), 3–4.

THE SEAL OF THE PROPHETS

1. Thomas Carlyle's description in "The Hero as Prophet," in *Heroes and Hero-Worship*, 1840. Reprint. (New York: Oxford University Press, 1974.)

2. Arabic has no neuter gender. As its nouns are invariably masculine or feminine, its pronouns are as well. In fidelity to the grammar of the Koran, therefore, I shall, when referring to Allah who possesses a masculine proper name, use the masculine pronoun.

3. See Charles Le Gai Eaton, *Islam and the Destiny of Man* (Albany: State University of New York Press, 1985), 103.

4. The literal meaning of the word *iqra'* is "recite," but here, where Muhammad was given his commission, I have followed the

trajectory of Victor Danner's "preach" (*The Islamic Tradition* [Amity, New York: Amity House, 1988], 35), but changed his word to "proclaim."

5. As rendered by Ameer Ali in *The Spirit of Islam*, 1902. Rev. ed. (London: Christophers, 1923), 18.

6. Ali, *Spirit of Islam*, 32.

7. Sir William Muir, quoted in Ali, *Spirit of Islam*, 32.

THE MIGRATION THAT LED TO VICTORY

1. Quoted without source in Ali, *Spirit of Islam*, 52.

2. Ali, *Spirit of Islam*, 52.

3. Philip Hitti, *The Arabs: A Short History*, 1949. Rev. ed. (New York: St. Martin's Press, 1968), 32.

4. Michael H. Hart, *The 100: A Ranking of the Most Influential Persons in History* (New York: Citadel Press, 1989), 40.

THE STANDING MIRACLE

1. Edward Gibbon, *The Decline and Fall of the Roman Empire*, 1845. Reprint. (New York: Modern Library, 1977), vol. 2, 162.

2. Today the language of Islam is a matter of sharp controversy. While all orthodox Muslims agree that the ritual use of the Koran in canonical prayers, and so on, must be in Arabic, there are many, including some among the *ulama* (religious scholars), who believe that on other occasions those who do not know Arabic should read the Koran in translation.

3. Kenneth Cragg, trans., *Readings in the Qur'an* (London: Collins, 1988), 18.

4. Frithjof Schuon, *Understanding Islam* (New York: Penguin Books, 1972), 44–45.

BASIC THEOLOGICAL CONCEPTS

1. "She [Mary] said: My Lord! How can I have a child when no mortal hath touched me? He [the angel] said: So. Allah createth what He will. If He decreeth a thing, He saith unto it only: Be! and it is" (3:47).

2. Tabari relates traditions on this episode that have God flattening the mountain with just his little finger.

3. Ali, *Spirit of Islam*, 150.

4. William James, *The Varieties of Religious Experience* (New York: Macmillan, 1961), 57.

5. Sir Muhammad Iqbal, *The Secrets of the Self,* 1920. Reprint. (Lahore: Muhammad Ashraf, 1979), xxi.

6. Quoted in Ali, *Spirit of Islam,* 199.

THE FIVE PILLARS

1. Ali, *Spirit of Islam,* 170.

2. Gai Eaton, *Islam and the Destiny of Man,* 55.

3. A *hadith of* the Prophet, reported in *Mishkat al-Masabih,* James Robson, trans. (Lahore: Sh. Muhammad Ashraf, 1965), 1264–67.

SOCIAL TEACHINGS

1. Bernard Lewis, *The Atlantic Monthly* (September 1990): 59.

2. Ali, *Spirit of Islam,* 173.

3. When I first revised this presentation in 1991, the Prime Minister of Pakistan and the leader of the opposition party in Bangladesh were both women. Muslim women could hold property in their own names from the start, whereas married women in the United States did not win that right until the twentieth century.

4. Outside slavery, we must add—a subject that, due to the variety of its local and historical forms, is too complex to consider here. See Bernard Lewis, *Race and Slavery in the Middle East* (New York: Oxford University Press, 1990).

5. Victor Danner, *The Islamic Tradition* (Amity, New York: Amity House, 1988), 131.

6. Kenneth Cragg, *The House of Islam* (Belmont, CA: Wadsworth, 1975), 122.

7. See Malcolm X, *The Autobiography of Malcolm X* (New York: Grove Press, 1964), 338–47.

8. Daniel, *Islam and the West,* 274.

9. Quoted by Ali, *Spirit of Islam,* 212.

10. Norman Daniel's *Islam and the West* supports them on this point.

SUFISM

1. *Hadith qudsi,* an extra-Koranic canonical saying of the Prophet, in which Allah speaks in the first person.

2. Cyprian Rice, *The Persian Sufis* (London: Allen & Unwin, 1964), 57.

3. The relation between mental and visionary knowledge is brought out in an exchange between the great Muslim philosopher Ibn Sina (Avicenna), and a contemporary ecstatic named Abu Sa'id. Ibn Sina said of Abu Sa'id, "What I know, he sees." Abu Sa'id returned the compliment. "What I see," he said, "he knows."

4. His actual words were, "I am the Truth," but Truth used here as one of the Ninety-nine Beautiful Names of Allah.

5. Idries Shah, *Tales of the Dervishes* (New York: E. P. Dutton, 1970), 23–24.